The Fix Your Credit Workbook

Also by Todd Bierman
(with Nathaniel Wice)

The Guerrilla Guide to Credit Repair

The
FIX YOUR CREDIT
Workbook

A Step-by-Step Guide to a Lifetime of Great Credit

TODD BIERMAN

and

DAVID MASTEN

ST. MARTIN'S Griffin

New York

Design by Susan Hood

Library of Congress Cataloging-in-Publication Data

Bierman, Todd.
    The fix-your-credit workbook : a step-by-step guide to a life-time of great credit / Todd Bierman & David Masten.
      p.   cm.
    ISBN 0-312-15530-1
    1. Consumer credit—United States.   2. Finance, Personal—United States.   I. Masten, David.   II. Title.
HG3756.U54B49   1998
332.7'43—DC21   97-12114
                                          CIP

10 9 8 7 6

CONTENTS

ACKNOWLEDGMENTS

———

The authors would like to thank the following people, whose work and patience have been invaluable in the creation of this book.

Edward J. Martz, Esq. (212) 563-0721. If you would like to hire an attorney to intercede on your behalf with creditors or file suit, we recommend him. Mr. Martz is an expert on credit law and speaks on behalf of the New York State Bar Association regarding credit. His consultation and contributions helped make the legal section of this book into a powerful tool. He was instrumental in the creation of the summons and complaints and gave direction to our explanation of the legal process. His offices are located at 450 Seventh Avenue, New York, N.Y. 10123.

Andrew Quick and Tom Quinn (ImageNet,N.Y.). (212) 388-9677. We would like to give special thanks to these gentlemen and this advertising firm, also located in New York City. They were a constant source of great ideas and creative fire. We were always made to feel welcome, and received the same attention and respect given their larger clients.

We would like to mention a few others who made this book project possible: John Masten Robert, Toba and Brad Bierman, Charlie Parshley, Kevin Cleary, Mrs. E. Ryan, Michelle Perez-Masten, David Weil, and countless others, including our clients, whose experiences and strength made it possible for us to see and report on successful credit negotiation.

George Witte and his assistants. Our editor and his highly professional staff were always there to bring this project forward. Thanks for their consistent, common-sense advice and support.

This book is dedicated to David's mother, Peggy Masten, who started him on his quest for credit information. She will be missed: February 14, 1995.

INTRODUCTION:
HOW THIS BOOK WORKS

―

 This workbook introduces you to the most powerful legal methods of repairing credit—negotiating for an *unrated account*. An unrated account is neither good nor bad and doesn't affect your credit rating. Though many credit repair texts detail how to conduct disputes with credit bureaus, our focus is on working directly with your creditors. This approach is advantageous because a creditor's agreement to change how your account is reported will simultaneously fix your credit at all three major credit bureaus, and is likely to do so in less than five weeks.

We map out the exact process of negotiating with creditors, one step at a time. From ordering and reading your reports, to analyzing your debts and negotiating to settle both money and credit-reporting issues, the book provides complete background information and proven settlement strategies. At each milestone, there are worksheets to track and organize your progress.

BACKGROUND INFORMATION

Chapter 1 is a series of frequently asked questions and answers on credit, credit reporting, and credit repair. These give you an understanding of the credit industry and help you prepare for the tasks ahead. Also included in this chapter are industry terms and definitions.

If you don't already have copies of recent credit reports, Chapter 2, "How to Get Your Credit Report," shows you how to get them. If you need to learn what the report says, Chapter 3, "How to Read Your Credit Report," explains the meaning behind the all-important *account status* section.

Don't assume that each report contains the same information—get all three. We've included all the information and letters you'll need to accomplish this goal. If you need to get a copy of your report from any of the bureaus in a hurry, you can alternatively call the authors. See Authors' Services (pages 4–6).

Next we help you establish a picture of your financial position. Chapter 4 gives you fill-in-the-blank financial charts to record what you owe, calculate what you have, and track your progress in preparation for future negotiations.

Chapter 5, "Negotiation," gives you more information about unrated accounts. We teach you how to conduct credit negotiations, including specific questions to ask, and what to expect from collection agents.

Alternatives to credit repair come next. Chapter 6 gives you information on bankruptcy and services available if you decide not to repair your credit. We suggest, however, that you use these options as a last resort.

Finally, depending on your success with your creditor negotiations, you'll decide if you have to use a lawsuit. Included in Chapter 7 are a set of questionnaires that will help you pinpoint which laws creditors, collection agents, or credit bureaus may have violated. After deciding which laws may have been violated, you will then be able to choose which of the four summons and complaints applies to your case. The next step is to fill out the complaint and send it to the defendant, including a cover letter from Chapter 8 that gives a brief, plain English interpretation of your legal dispute. The cover letter we give you includes the term *notice of claim*. Labeling an unfiled lawsuit as a notice of claim is a legal way of presenting your intent to sue without the defendant being able credibly to say you are attempting to extort a favorable settlement. If you were to tell the defendant, "If I don't get my way I will sue you," your actions could be interpreted as a threat of legal process, which is illegal. By labeling your actions as a notice of claim, you are, in the eyes of the court, giving the defendant an opportunity to cure the error. This admittedly technical point is important to the processes described in this book, because you may have to send copies of summons and complaints to your opponent in order to get his or her attention. Many creditors grease only the squeakiest wheel, and your negotiations with customer service representatives may never reach the level where someone can actually make a command decision. A lawsuit or notice of claim, on the other hand, certainly gets attention and will likely open him or her up to the idea of a settlement in an effort to avoid a courtroom confrontation.

CREDIT OVERVIEW

CREDIT: *Time given for payment of goods or services sold on trust, faith, belief, and honor. Financial trustworthiness. Authorization of a purchase based on trust.*

Credit is the American way. Our dreams and futures are based on it. Your college education is borrowed, home mortgaged, or car financed on it. The world we live in is dependent on credit and credit histories. So why aren't we taught about credit? Why isn't the information in this book readily available? One explanation is that the monied powers behind credit would prefer that you didn't know. The system depends on dealing with the public as individuals, each needing to learn the ropes on his or her own. If every American knew that credit was negotiable, the relatively inflexible system would fail. It depends on a flock of willing, regular payers who do so without question.

Credit reporting as we know it is outlawed in most European countries, where the practice of reporting private consumer financial history is known as *blacklisting*. Despite the lack of reporting, their banking systems seem to thrive. Unfortunately for Americans, major defense contractors such as TRW (now renamed *Experian*) have great political clout, making the demise of our credit system highly unlikely.

In recent years, overall consumer debt has grown, and with terrible consequences. More people than ever before are seeking bankruptcy as a solution to their debt. In 1980 approximately 350,000 personal bankruptcies were filed. By 1990 that number had doubled, and in 1997 it's closer to a million. Many of these individuals would have avoided bankruptcy if they'd had more information on credit, how it's reported, and how it can be negotiated. We methodically teach this information here.

Whether you owe one creditor or many, you can take the offensive and force a settlement of your debt while getting clear credit in the bargain. We teach you how to exercise power and leverage. The power is in negotiation and skillful use of the law. The leverage is that only you can pay. Without your paying, the creditor loses.

Unfortunately, most debtors eventually pay without negotiating for clear credit, possibly out of fear, honor, or ignorance. In the worst cases, they go bankrupt. We suggest that you fight rather than fold. If someone is coming after you, it is your obligation to defend yourself and do it well, preserving what is yours to the fullest extent available within the law. That is how the other side plays, and simply by recognizing that you are playing hardball, you've cleared the first hurdle to fixing your credit.

Other Publications from the Authors and Authors' Services

INTRODUCTION TO OUR FIRST CREDIT BOOK, *THE GUERRILLA GUIDE TO CREDIT REPAIR*

The Guerrilla Guide to Credit Repair goes into detail on reading and interpreting credit reports, and disputing credit reporting with the credit bureaus. The *Guide* deals with the most common dispute method—sending letter after letter to the credit bureaus. While this works, many who employ it do so in violation of the law. The common credit repair scam is to deny true credit information and win by process. The bureaus simply can't keep up with their end of the confirmation rules under the Fair Credit Reporting Act, and so they delete the negative credit because they can't meet the time constraints imposed by the law.

The *Guide* allows you to use the dispute method, but instead of denying the truth, you bring up legitimate questions concerning finer points of the Fair Credit Reporting and Fair Billing acts. By calling into question the process used by creditors to assert their version of your credit history, the letter dispute method can be used effectively and legally in many cases.

The Fix Your Credit Workbook deals entirely with negotiating how credit is reported, taking over where the *Guide* left off with legal remedies and documents that enable any consumer to carry on a forceful effort at rapidly clearing up credit reporting at its source—the creditor. This is the method commonly employed by attorneys.

While the *Workbook* is effective at the most powerful method of credit repair, you may want to learn the methods detailed in the *Guide* because some credit problems can be dealt with more quickly by circumventing creditors and going straight to the credit bureaus. The cases where this is true are noted in the *Workbook,* with the necessary documents included in those sections. Taken together, the *Guide* and the *Workbook* complement each other well, creating the most complete source of information on understanding and executing effective, legal credit repair.

Credit Insider Magazine

Credit Insider Magazine is the newest publication from best-selling credit authors David Masten and Todd Bierman. *CI* is for the general public—those who want to understand, build, and improve their credit rating. For the first time, this information is offered from an unbiased source not beholden to the credit industry. Subscribers to this quarterly publication also have exclusive access to the *Insider* Web site. In addition to providing time-sensitive news, data, and legal information, the Web site has a complete library for dealing with a wide variety of credit issues. There are additional letters and forms that can be downloaded and customized for purposes ranging from correcting problems to making money and expanding your financial world.

The combination of the publication and Web site gives you updated lists of the best bank rates, the newest, most competitive credit card offerings, sources of credit data and reports, an extensive credit library, and a widely praised question-and-answer forum that builds on the extensive knowledge contained in *CI*—all delivered in fast-paced, easy-to-read style.

QUESTION AUTHORITY

CI has a staff of attorneys recognized for their expertise in credit law. Our years of practical experience provide you with priceless information previously unavailable to the general public. As the first and only news source featuring unbiased information on the consumer credit reporting industry, we haven't always made friends with the big guys. The huge companies that report credit supposedly operate under the strict rule of law. As with any inflexible system, they depend on a willing flock of unquestioning consumers. Week by week, *CI* gives you the breaking news, court precedents, and proven techniques to get the most out of the credit-reporting process. Simply put, credit bureaus could avoid working for you—until now. Consumers and lending professionals can demand the best from creditors and credit bureaus. *Credit Insider Magazine* delivers.

Authors' Services

The following services are also available from the authors. Call for current pricing.

- Legal forms, customized
- Credit reports, consumer and infile versions

- Referral for legitimate consumer credit counseling
- Information on legal services

To order *The Guerrilla Guide to Credit Repair*, ask your bookseller or order directly from the authors.
- $8.95 (U.S. dollars) plus $3.50 for shipping and handling. Orders will be shipped out for two-day delivery by the U.S. Postal Service.

To order *Credit Insider Magazine*:
- 1-year subscription and Web access, $125.00

Phone orders can be made using Visa, MasterCard, American Express, or Discover by calling (800) 561-6685.

FOR MAIL ORDERS

Make checks payable to *Credit Insider Magazine*:

Credit Insider Magazine
160 5th Avenue
Suite 911
New York, NY 10010

1.

FREQUENTLY ASKED QUESTIONS AND ANSWERS

———

 This chapter contains many of the frequently asked questions on credit repair, credit bureaus, and credit negotiation. If you need to orient yourself on how the process described in this book works and find the best direction for your repair efforts, start here.

Q: *Where do I start?*
A: Following the path marked out in this book, get a copy of your recent credit history to get a substantially accurate picture of what you owe (Chapter 2, "How to Get Your Credit Report"). If you have debt problems, figure out your ability and the order in which to repay your creditors (Chapter 4, "Prioritize Your Debts," page 25). After determining how or whether to pay your creditors, make a tactical plan on negotiating settlements that includes a clean credit history. If you need to use more persuasive methods than offering payment, review your legal rights by completing the questionnaires on pages 65–74. If you find them violated, send your creditor a summons and complaint (Chapter 7, "Legal Section") that details your grievance and asks for a settlement of clear credit.

Q: *What are the hardest credit items to fix, in order of difficulty?*
A: The three most difficult are tax liens, student loans, and judgments because of the effort it takes to force these items from a report.

1. *Tax liens.* The government doesn't make credit reporting deals. Credit laws such as the Fair Credit Reporting Act don't have jurisdiction over government

agencies. You've got to pay your liens, with the understanding that so many individuals have satisfied liens on their report that using this against you in a lending decision would be unusual.

2. *Student loans.* Though these often originate at a bank, they are generally backed by the U.S. government. If you default on the loan, the government won't fix the problem. Since paid loan information is often archived, conducting a credit bureau dispute is often the best way to get rid of derogatory student loan information. Despite your best efforts at dealing with the intricacies of student loans, the loan agencies are disorganized (at best) and often fail to correct their collection errors. The disorganization works in your favor, because once a loan is fully paid, the loan agencies have difficulty finding older data on fully paid loans and fail to meet the deadlines specified in credit reporting laws on confirming or denying your dispute. The credit bureaus must delete any item that is unconfirmed after thirty to forty-five days.

3. *Judgments.* Items in the public record, such as judgments, can be removed by repeated letters to credit bureaus denying their validity, especially if you have solid evidence for your position. If you still owe on the judgment, you can negotiate with your opponent's attorney to get an agreement that he or she will *stand still* after you pay the debt so that you can file a motion to dismiss judgment. After you file it, and your opponent fails to answer the motion, the judgment will be dismissed. Though the original judgment will exist, the dismissal is also on your credit report. Alternatively, you might even get the opposing attorney to agree to a stipulation that the judgment be dismissed upon your payment.

4. *Foreclosures.* You will likely have to wait seven years to get this off your report, unless you dispute with the credit bureaus and they are unable to confirm it. You may want to consider forfeiting your *deed in-lieu-of foreclosure,* meaning that you voluntarily give up your house. Alternatively, filing bankruptcy can buy you time to reorganize your debt, stalling off foreclosure. See Chapter 6, "Alternatives to Credit Repair."

5. *Repossession.* Again, you may have to wait seven years for this to leave your report. Rather than allow the repossession to occur, you may consider a *voluntary surrender* of your car instead of incurring a more negative *repossession* rating.

Q: *What is a credit bureau?*

A: There are actually two main types of credit bureaus. Huge companies such as TRW (now called Experian), Equifax, and Trans Union are the main repositories of consumer credit information, each of them holding records on approximately 150 million Americans. The other class of credit bureaus is comprised of thousands of small, independent companies that provide credit reports to lenders on a more local level. Often these small operators combine reports from either two or all three of the main repositories to get a more complete picture of your credit background or to fulfill mortgage lending laws that require a combination of at least two repositories.

No matter where your credit is reported from, the laws that govern reporting are the same for all agencies, whether the original reporter of the information or a smaller rereporter. In fact, legally challenging the smaller bureaus can be more effective than going after a giant company, because smaller bureaus can make reporting changes much more quickly and are less capable of withstanding costly legal proceedings.

Q: *What are the components of a credit report?*
A: Credit profiles have four main parts.

1. *Personal information.* This includes name, address, previous address, date of birth, and social security number.

2. *Account information.* This section has credit accounts and loans, including when they were opened, how they were paid (on time or not), how much you owe, the credit limit, if the account is shared or not, and the account status (telling, for example, if the account is in collection or has been declared a charge-off).

3. *Public records.* Include tax liens, judgments, and bankruptcies.

4. *Inquiries.* Who has requested a report on you. Though inquiries generally stay on your report for two years, they can remain longer if you don't request that the old ones be removed. (See Chapter 3, "How to Read Your Credit Report.")

Q: *What are my rights if I'm turned down for credit?*
A: The denying creditor must tell you the reason for rejection, and if a credit report was involved in the decision, who issued it. You're also entitled to a free report from this reporting bureau, whose name appears on the creditor's rejection letter.

Q: *How long will bad credit stay on my credit report?*
A: Unless you negotiate as we teach, most items will remain for seven years from the time they are reported by your creditor. The exceptions are bank-

ruptcies, which remain for ten years from the date they are settled, and judgments, which remain for up to twenty years if unsettled.

Q: *Do rejections hurt my credit rating?*
A: Yes. The more rejections you have on your report, even if the cause of the rejection was an error that has been corrected, the more difficult it is to get credit. Every time you apply for credit, an *inquiry* appears on your report. Though more complete credit reports will indicate whether the inquiry resulted in rejection, most reports don't. Some lenders assume that many inquiries mean many rejections.

Q: *What if there are inquiries on my report from companies I don't recognize?*
A: Credit bureaus sell your name to businesses for marketing purposes. These marketing inquiries are generally differentiated from credit application inquiries. You needn't worry about them. Still, you should be aware that merely talking to some businesses about their credit products will cause them to pull a report. This is legal if they have a genuine belief that they might extend you credit. Some auto and mortgage lenders are particularly aggressive in this gray area of *belief.* When in doubt, clearly tell them not to pull a report until you authorize it in writing. You can dispute inquiries directly with credit bureaus, and they are often removed. A sample of an inquiry dispute is included in Chapter 8, "Letters."

Q: *How am I judged by a lending institution?*
A: Lenders generally use scoring systems to rate consumers when considering loan applications. They get credit scores from outside, independent sources, or they may use an in-house rating system. Credit bureaus have rated consumers for many years, but until 1992 the bureaus didn't reveal that a rating system existed. The Federal Trade Commission (FTC) now requires credit bureaus to disclose credit risk scores and their meaning to consumers on request.

There are two main types of scoring systems used in approving credit applications. The first is called a *judgmental evaluation system.* A creditor looks at each application individually using set guidelines that take into account your credit history and income versus debt. In this increasingly rare system, lenders use their best judgment to arrive at a credit-granting decision.

The second rating system is *numerical credit scoring.* Here your application is compared to past lending data and statistically analyzed to determine the risk in extending you credit. Your score is based on your answers to application questions and your credit history. The bottom line is that a computer analyzes your application instead of a person.

How does this scoring system work? The creditor will identify a number of factors such as length and type of employment, income, and credit payment history. Each topic reviewed is assigned a point value. For example, if you are a professional (doctor, lawyer, CEO), you may get 8 points. If you are self-employed, you might get 1 point. A past bankruptcy might be a −10. The lending institution establishes a cutoff score, say 15, under which you are automatically rejected. Some lenders may review a rejected application if a score falls close to the cutoff point (13–15) and employ a judgmental evaluation. Others rely on a computer from start to finish.

Most credit card application reviews start with a computer. The only human interaction is data entry. Even the rejection letters are automated. While debate continues about the merits of relying solely on automated systems, there is objective evidence that removing human judgment from the decision process is the most effective way to avoid making bad loans. Sears reportedly discovered that deviating from their automated scoring system dramatically increased lending defaults.

Many aspects of credit scoring seem contrary to common sense. For example, paying all your bills on time or having lots of clean credit available should make you a good credit risk. If, however, you take a lot of cash advances from your credit cards, you may be placed in a higher risk category in spite of your highly responsible repayment record. The credit-reporting agencies also score you on other borrowing behavior, the profitability of your account, and the chance that you might file bankruptcy in the near future. For more information on credit scoring, see Chapter 9, "More Credit Topics."

Q: *If I want to stop a collection agent from pestering me, what do I do?*
A: Under the Fair Debt Collection Practices Act, you can write to a collection agency, inform it that you will not honor its collection attempts, and it can no longer contact you for the purpose of settling the debt. See the cease collection letter on page 117.

Q: *If I owe creditors money and can't pay, how do I buy time?*
A: The first method of gaining some time is to ask for a complete accounting in writing of what you owe. A request for billing *clarification* is technically a

billing error. If a creditor takes, for example, three weeks to answer your request, you have an equal amount of time in which to pay. Should you believe that a charge on your credit card bill is incorrect, you have sixty days from the time you are billed to make your dispute.

After your creditor has conducted its investigation and answered your request, it has fulfilled its obligations. The only way you could further the dispute process is by actually filing a lawsuit. Don't do this unless you truly believe you are justified and can provide some evidence for your position.

Occasionally, a creditor will grant you a grace period in which you don't have to keep up with regular payments, and it won't report derogatory credit. Usually, though, it makes an agreement to accept reduced payments but to report late payments on the account. Essentially, the creditor agrees not to send the account into collections, or close it, because you have contacted it and sought a new agreement. If you seek and obtain an agreement for deferred or reduced payments, you must clearly define the terms on this altered payment plan, including how credit reporting will be affected. Often you need to get someone at a management level to make this type of agreement. Don't be shy about asking for the boss.

Q: *What is credit repair?*

A: There are three main types of credit repair:

1. *Credit bureau letter campaign.* Write letter after letter to the credit bureaus asking them to remove the bad credit item. This method is illegal if you are using the U.S. mail or a phone to make statements that you know are not true—it's mail or wire fraud. If you think you are in the right, credit bureau letters can be effective at repairing credit. Still, going directly to the source of the problem, your creditor, is usually a more effective method of repairing your credit in a short period of time, though it requires slightly more effort because you need to conduct a series of negotiations. You need to enforce the new creditor agreements by writing the credit bureaus and asking them to change your account. We include the appropriate credit bureau dispute letters for doing this in Chapter 8, "Letters."

2. *New report method.* This involves using a variation on your name and another social security/tax ID number to open a second credit record that is unblemished. You may get a visit from the FBI for doing this. The method for creating this *split file* is widely published as a quick cure-all for your credit problems. Don't get suckered into it.

3. *Negotiation and settlement.* Approaching each creditor who's given you a bad credit history and using an offer to settle your debts (backed by a workable payment plan) and/or a legitimate threat of legal action for any of the many possible technical violations it may have made under federal or state credit laws may convince it to report nothing about your account (see Questionnaire 1, page 65, to identify technical violations). This is effective because reporting nothing is neither illegal, a lie, nor extraordinary—it's done all the time. We show the way to this goal in detail. There are some creditors, such as the government, and derogatory credit, such as public records, where negotiation is impossible. You may want to consider the credit bureau dispute method.

Q: *If I do have a lawsuit, do I go to court?*
A: Not necessarily. Just presenting your lawsuit along with a letter demanding settlement of your debts and credit record simultaneously may be enough. You might have to file the lawsuit to bring the other side to the table, and if you have sufficient knowledge of legal process, you can see the matter through to a trial. Still, we suggest that if you do go to court, consult a competent attorney.

CREDIT TERMS AND DEFINITIONS

Account status. A term such as *paid account,* meaning that you owe nothing, or *was 30,* which indicates that you were late but are now current. This status term is as close to a credit account rating as most consumers get. Remember: Any status term that indicates anything other than a perfect, on-time account is not good credit.

Bankruptcy. A court-ordered plan that protects consumers from their creditors while they either establish a new repayment plan for their debts (Chapter 13 bankruptcy) or liquidate their assets to pay all or some of their total debts (Chapter 7 bankruptcy). (See Chapter 6, "Alternatives to Credit Repair.")

Bankruptcy discharge. The act of completing a bankruptcy, either by liquidating assets in a Chapter 7, or finishing a modified debt repayment plan in Chapter 13 bankruptcy.

Charge-off. Also known as a *profit and loss write-off,* this extremely bad credit account status labels you as a deadbeat who won't pay. Most creditors are obligated to report sufficiently delinquent accounts in this way, because it directly affects their shareholder profitability.

Collateral. Items such as a house or car that a lending institution uses as the basis for extending a loan. If the loan is not repaid, the collateral is seized.

Collection account. An account turned over from your creditor to a third-party collection agency. From the time the account goes to collection, it may be reported as bad credit for seven years.

Consumer. The legal term used to identify an individual.

Consumer report. A written, oral, or other communication of any information by a consumer reporting agency bearing on a consumer's creditworthiness.

Cosigner. A person who guarantees credit that is extended to you, by offering his or her own credit, money, or property as collateral. If you do not repay the debt, the cosigner will have to. The cosigner's credit is affected by the repayment history of the loan, bad or good.

Credit bureau. Also known as a *consumer reporting agency,* a company that collects and reports credit information. It sells your information to third parties for the purpose of extending you credit.

Credit counselor. An employee of a company licensed to negotiate debts with creditors and administer a repayment plan, unlike an unlicensed credit consultant.

Credit file. Information on a consumer's payment history recorded and retained by a consumer reporting agency.

Creditor. A lender.

Credit repair service. A company that conducts disputes and negotiations with credit bureaus and creditors. Though there are legitimate credit repair services, there are many charlatans in this business. Generally, credit repair companies are not allowed to charge up front for their repair services, though they may charge a consulting fee. Exercise caution when hiring a repair service.

Credit score. A method used by a lending institution to judge your creditworthiness. The method used differs from lender to lender, but all base their decisions on some of the following: income, how long have you been at your job, how long have you lived at your home, whether you pay your bills on time or have revolving credit.

Debit card. A bank card that looks like a Visa or MasterCard and can be used anywhere that accepts these cards, but it has a credit line tied to a bank account.

Defendant. The person who defends himself or herself against an allegation of wrongdoing in a lawsuit.

Demand letter. A letter sent to any business or person demanding rectification of a dispute. In some circumstances, a demand letter is a necessary first step in beginning a legal action because you must give the other party in a dispute an opportunity to cure the problem.

Discretionary income. The money you have left after paying all your debts in a given time period.

Equity loan. A loan secured on the value of an investment such as a home, stocks, or artwork that is pledged as collateral. In the event that the loan is not repaid, the home, for example, could be foreclosed on to repay the debt.

Fair Credit Reporting Act (FCRA). The law that governs creation and dissemination of consumer credit reports.

Financial statement. A document that lists all your assets, income, and debts.

Forced liquidation. A lower value on an asset than market value, often used by the IRS to satisfy a tax lien.

Foreclosure. The repossession of real estate property by a lender.

Freezing debt. Getting your creditor to stop the accrual of interest on a debt, usually done as part of a modified repayment plan.

Full factual report. A credit report issued by a company that actually verifies all the income, residence, and employment information, usually by phone.

Grace period. The time that a lender gives you to make a payment beyond the official deadline, wherein you can pay back your debt and not owe interest, penalties, or incur bad credit.

Infile. A credit report, differentiated from a *consumer report* because it often contains more detailed information on your account history. It is generally presented in a more detailed and encoded format useful to lending professionals. (See Chapter 3, "How to Read Your Credit Report.")

Inquiries. A record of every company that has seen your credit report in the past two years. Each listing is called a inquiry. Too many inquiries on your report may affect your ability to obtain credit, because this suggests that you've been repeatedly denied credit.

Installment credit. Credit extended and paid on a regular basis in a fixed amount.

Judgment. A court order that you owe a creditor money, which allows it a number of legal methods of seizing your assets. A judgment stays on your report for seven years after it has been paid. If you don't pay, it may stay on your report for as long as twenty years. (You can check the statute of limitations with your state attorney general's office.)

Jurisdiction. The territory in which a particular court has the right to make binding legal decisions. In the case of federal laws covered in this book, the entire United States is within the jurisdiction of a federal court.

Liability. An obligation to a lender.

Obligor. A person who owes money to a creditor.

Obsolete information. Any information on a credit report older than seven years. Exceptions are *bankruptcies* (ten years) and *judgments* (which run the length of the statute of limitations, generally twenty years). In practice, obsolete information may remain on your report until you send a letter to all three credit bureaus asking for deletion.

Plaintiff. The person who initiates a lawsuit.

Public records. These include tax liens, judgments, and bankruptcies. They are usually collected for credit bureaus by companies that go to the courthouse, gather this information, and sell it.

Return receipt. A green card attached to certified mail, which is signed by the receiver and sent back to the sender as proof that the letter was delivered, or *served* as a legal document in a court case.

Revolving credit. Credit extended and paid on a monthly basis with a minimum payment and a total amount due, both of which can fluctuate.

Secured credit card. Offered to consumers with bad credit or no credit. It is approved on the basis of a savings account that will be the security for repayment. (See Authors' Services, pages 4–6, for information on the best secured card issuers.)

Split file. An additional, unblemished personal credit file usually created by deceptive means in an effort to gain credit.

Stand still. For the purposes of this book, an agreement with an opposing attorney not to fight your motion to dismiss a judgment, generally made on the condition that you pay the amount owed.

Summons and complaint. A legal form consisting of two parts. The first, the *summons*, commands the defendants of a lawsuit to answer your allegations of wrongdoing. The second, the *complaint,* is your version of the wrongdoing and your request of the court to grant you relief from those wrongs.

Tax lien. A city, state, or federal government judgment that allows the tax authorities to seize your real property or money.

Trustee. An individual appointed by the court to oversee the administration of payments to creditors in a bankruptcy.

Unsecured creditor. A creditor who has loaned money or merchandise without a legal right to collateral in cases where the obligor failed to pay.

U.S.C. United States Code. A legal term prefacing sections of federal law.

Voluntary surrender. An *account status* term used in credit reporting when you turn over a vehicle that you can no longer afford payments on.

2.

HOW TO GET YOUR CREDIT REPORT

The first step necessary in fixing your credit is to see how it's reported. There are three major bureaus that collect and resell credit information. They are TRW (now called Experian), Trans Union, and Equifax. It's important to see what each of them says about you. It's a mistake to assume that a report from one is the same as the others, so get all three.

Understanding what type of report you have is important. Most consumers receive a consumer version that is less complete than professional reports known as *infiles*. A combination report containing credit histories from two bureaus is called a *full factual* or *residential mortgage credit report*. Learn how to identify and read the different credit reports in Chapter 3, "How to Read Your Credit Report."

STEPS TO GET YOUR REPORT

The following are examples of how to receive your credit report and make a determination if it's free or not. If time is a factor, the authors offer a report service. See page 5 for more information.

If you have applied for credit and were recently rejected, you are entitled to a free report from the bureau that supplied the information that resulted in credit denial. Send a copy of the creditor's rejection letter, along with your full name including any middle initial, a copy of some type of picture ID, current

18

address and previous address covering the past five years, a copy of either your driver's license, social security card, or a bill sent to your home address, and request a report.

TRW/Experian used to send out free reports once a year to any consumer requesting one. No more. All credit bureaus will, however, send a free report as part of a credit item dispute resolution process. It is your obligation to check all three bureaus, because you can't assume they report identical information.

There is an $8.00 charge to get your report from Experian, Equifax, or Trans Union, if you haven't been denied credit based on any of these companies' reports. Certain states grant consumers the right to get reports for less money. Inquire about fees using the 800 numbers below.

All three credit bureaus take as many as thirty days to respond to your inquiries and requests.

TRW/Experian
(800) 392-1122
If you have been denied credit by this company, send all information to:
  Experian
  Box 2104
  Allen, TX 75013-2104
Note: Over the last few years, Experian (formerly TRW) has changed its exact mailing address a number of times. Although the general request address is always in Allen, Texas, the box number changes. There may be good reasons for the switch, but one bad result for consumers is that the company can disregard whole batches of free report requests because they were sent to the wrong location.

Trans Union
(800) 916-8800
If you have been denied credit by this company, you can use its voice request system. If you are requesting a report and have not been denied credit, send all information to:
  Trans Union
  760 Sproul Road
  Box 403
  Springfield, PA 19064

Equifax Information Service
(800) 685-1111
If you have been denied credit by this company or are requesting a copy of a credit report, send information to :

Equifax Information Service
Attention: Consumer Correspondence
Box 740256
Atlanta, GA 30374-0193

PROTECT YOURSELF

When you send these letters, and all other letters in this workbook, always do the following:

- Use certified/return receipt mail. It's an excellent method of proving that you sent the letter and it was received.
- Keep a copy of everything you send.
- Make a note of the date you sent your request. If you haven't received your report within four weeks from the send date, send another letter to the bureau and pencil in a note that you will notify the Federal Trade Commission of the company's failure to send your credit report in a timely fashion. The law requires the bureaus to supply you with your credit report and to do so within forty-five days from receipt of your written request.

3.

HOW TO READ YOUR CREDIT REPORT

―――

 Credit reports are difficult for civilians to read because they were originally designed for professional use. Because more consumers have access to their reports, credit bureaus have reluctantly moved toward making them easier to read. Even so, most people don't understand their credit report. This is unlikely to change soon because the bureaus know you can't dispute what you don't understand.

There are many different credit report styles, but they are all derived from information reported by the three major bureaus. Each bureau has different instructions for reading its reports, but all reports contain the following information.

- Creditor name/Type of creditor
- Account number
- Status of account
- Lateness patterns

The back of most consumer credit reports contains a brief explanation of its contents. The bureaus also publish, for an additional fee, a more complete booklet on this subject. The encoded reports dissuade consumers from challenging their credit histories and offer ineffective repair advice at best. The newer plain-English reporting style actually offers less information than previous reports. The bottom line: Credit bureaus aren't working for consumers.

TYPES OF CREDIT REPORTS

Infiles

Not all credit reports contain the same information. The reports lenders generally see are called *infiles,* which contain more detailed account information than a consumer report, especially when it comes to derogatory credit. TRW/Experian assigns a national risk score ranging from 0 to 1,000 (0–70 indicating good credit) that is conveniently excluded from consumer reports. Also missing are letter codes that explain the reasons behind your score.

Full Factual/Residential Mortgage Credit Reports

A *full factual report* is a special report used to evaluate mortgage applications. It is a compilation of at least two credit bureaus' records. The full factual report also includes information on the applicant's employment, income, and residence, among other details of a credit application, and it is verified by an employee of the credit compiler that issues the report.

Consumer Disclosure

These are reports sent by credit bureaus in response to an individual's request. TRW's consumer disclosure reduces the codes and abbreviations of professional reports to plain English. Unfortunately, the result is so sanitized that no creditor could make a lending decision on the limited information. Trans Union's consumer report is more similar to its professional version than either Experian or Equifax, though Equifax comes close to Trans Union in completeness. In general, consumer disclosures are either limited or encoded, both yielding the same result: You usually doesn't learn what your credit history says.

READING CONSUMER DISCLOSURE AND INFILES

The most important sections of any credit report are the *account status* and the *payment history*. The following is a summary on reading the three credit bureaus' reports.

TRW/Experian

On consumer disclosures, Experian attempts to explain facts such as: you are responsible for your account, that you owe a certain amount of money, and whether you've been late, though it doesn't tell you when. It is exactly this type of omission that makes repairing errant credit challenging. Without knowing exactly when you've been marked late, it is difficult to dispute your credit.

Example of Experian account status statement:

> This open account is current and all payments are being made on time, but was 60 days late during the reporting history. Scheduled monthly payments: 57.00, last payment reported to Experian: 5/97 Account Balance: 1,057.00 on 5/97. Months previewed: 84.

The right-hand column of an actual Experian infile has the following information:

> Cur-Was 60.
> nnnccccccc12
> nncc1nnncccc

"Cur-Was 60" indicates that *a current account was sixty days late sometime within the last seven years.* The letter and number codes indicate payment history, with the first *n* representing account status twenty-four months ago, and the last *c* representing the month the report was issued. The letter *n* means nothing was owed on the account. A *c* means money was owed and was paid on time. A 1 means that payment was one month late. The 2 following the 1 means that there was a second month in which payment wasn't made.

The account status "Cur - Was 60" describes late paying history. Even if all the letter codes in this most recent twenty-four months are *c*, that is, paid on time, the account could still list "Was 60" because the derogatory status reflects the last seven years. The reporting of codes for the last twenty-four months, coupled with an account status reflecting much older late marks, confuses almost everyone.

Trans Union

This is an example of both the consumer disclosure and infile:

```
111111211111
111X11111111
47 0 0 1
```

Again, the twenty-four numbers/letters in the top two lines represent the last twenty-four months. The first 1 indicates twenty-four months ago, and the last 1 refers to the current month. The number 1 on this report means paid on time; a 2 means thirty days late. The account status numbers on the third line indicate that credit has been reported for forty-seven months on this account, there are 0 ninety-day late payments, 0 sixty-day lates, and 1 thirty-day late payment.

Equifax Information Service

>>>30(1) 60 (1) 90(0) 7/95-R2<<<

This notation indicates that the account has been thirty days late on one occasion, sixty days late on one occasion, and never ninety days late. The additional note, *7/95-R2*, tells the date of the sixty-day late. An R1 can designate both an on-time and a thirty-day-late account. Here again, there's no telling when the thirty-day late occurred. This most certainly is a bad credit report, and it makes disputes quite difficult. Note that Equifax gives an account history only when there is negative credit.

If, after reading your report, you still don't get it, see Authors' Services (pages 4–6) to subscribe to *Credit Insider Magazine*. Subscribers can E-mail the site for specific advice. The *Insider* Web site also has copies of all the documents in this book among a complete library of reference materials. These documents can be downloaded as text files, making them easy to customize with any PC word-processing application.

4.

YOUR FINANCIAL POSITION

PRIORITIZE YOUR DEBTS

TRIAGE: *The act of choosing among the wounded to decide the order in which they will receive care.*

In catastrophes, triage is used to save lives. The decision maker decides who receives attention first according to the extent of the injuries. The person with the worst injuries is usually treated first, the next worst is treated second, and so on. Sometimes, the injury is so bad that resources are best used elsewhere. We suggest you apply the theory of triage to your credit problems. Whom do you pay, or not, and in what order? Making this decision depends on whom you owe as well as how much. Sometimes an account can't be made whole again, and your resources are better used elsewhere. The goal of this chapter is to triage your debts.

WHERE TO START

The first step is to get organized. We include a number of forms to record all your income, assets, debts, payments, and arrears, giving you a clear picture of where you stand. The work you do in this chapter is a first round at organizing your debts. Deciding which debts are most important to settle is an ongoing process. After you learn how to order your attack, read Chapter 5, "Negotiation." You may find after beginning your negotiations that some of your first assumptions were wrong. You'll likely need to keep reordering your priorities as you proceed. Rarely have we worked through an entire set of debt negotiations without discovering new issues. Some creditors may have a different debt figure in mind from the one you assumed. Some may resist because you've already had a few chances, and they won't grant yet another. Other creditors you assume are going to be difficult may roll over and accept your offer simply because it is part of a well-considered plan.

FILLING OUT THE FORMS

Start the process by getting your account information in order. You need copies of your recent creditor statements and credit reports to fill out the account forms in this chapter. Feel free to photocopy the forms for reuse. Each form includes space to record what you owe, your last monthly payment, your arrears, and credit bureau account rating (known as account status).

Account status terms on the forms are summaries for a wide variety of terms on your credit report. For example, *was late* stands for any thirty-, sixty-, or ninety-day lateness you had on your report in the last seven years. *Judgment* includes all liens and public records.

You'll also see a space to fill in the *debt priority* #. This gives you an order for working with creditors, since the process of negotiating a number of debts can be lengthy and cumbersome. Over time, as you learn more, and settle certain debts, you may want to change the priority number.

You should fill out the account identification, financial, and credit-reporting sections of this form now. You'll fill out the negotiation contact information after reading that section and actually beginning your negotiations.

Personal Information

Because of the disjointed nature of credit negotiations, it may be necessary for you to answer questions about a second party if you get a call back from a creditor and, for example, your spouse isn't available. This page will allow you to have personal data on yourself, your spouse, or possibly a cosigner-signer on a loan, all on one page. No matter who answers the phone, or who is present when you actually get through to the right person in your creditor's organization, you'll have empowered anyone who has a stake in the outcome of your attempt at clear credit to move the negotiation forward.

Personal Information Form

Your name _____

Billing address _____

_____

_____

Past or second address _____

_____

_____

Phone # _____

Date of birth _____

SS # _____

Mother's maiden name _____

Company _____

Company's phone # _____ Extension _____

Direct dial number, if different _____

Spouse's/Cosigner-signer's/Other's name _____

Billing address _____

Past or second address _____

Phone # _____

Date of birth _____

SS# _____

Mother's maiden name _____

Company _____

Company's phone # _____ Extension _____

Direct dial number, if different _____

Bank Credit Cards

Debt priority # _____

□ MasterCard □ Visa □ Amex
□ Discover □ Optima □ Other

Account Status

Account number _____

Lender name _____

Address _____

_____

□ Was late □ Charge off
□ Is late □ Judgment
□ Collection □ Closed

Date opened _____

Phone # (___) _____

Expiration date _____

Balance $_____ Annual percentage rate _____%

Minimum payment $_____ Credit limit $_____ Total interest owed $_____

PAYMENT HISTORY

Month/Year of last payment _____

How many payments have you missed _____

Total amount overdue (update every 30 days) _____

CONTACTS FOR NEGOTIATION

First Contact Person

Name _____ Direct Phone (____) _____

Address _____

Date of 1st contact _____ Outcome _____

Follow-up date _____

Date of 2nd contact _____ Outcome _____

Follow-up date _____

Date notice of claim sent _____ Date federal suit filed _____

Second Contact Person

Name _____ Direct Phone (____) _____

Address _____

Date of 1st contact _____ Outcome _____

Follow-up date _____

Date of 2nd contact _____ Outcome _____

Follow-up date _____

Notes _____

_____

Retail Credit Cards

Debt priority # _____

Account Status

☐ Was late ☐ Charge off

☐ Is late ☐ Judgment

Account number _____

☐ Collection

Lender name _____

Address _____

_____

Phone # (___) _____

Balance $_____ Annual percentage rate _____%

Minimum payment $_____ Credit limit $_____ Total interest owed $_____

PAYMENT HISTORY

Month/Year of last payment _____

How many payments have you missed _____

Total amount overdue (update every 30 days) _____

CONTACTS FOR NEGOTIATION

First Contact Person

Name _____ Direct Phone (____) _____

Address _____

Date of 1st contact _____ Outcome _____

Follow-up date _____

Date of 2nd contact _____ Outcome _____

Follow-up date _____

Date notice of claim sent _____ Date federal suit filed _____

Second Contact Person

Name _____ Direct Phone (____) _____

Address _____

Date of 1st contact _____ Outcome _____

Follow-up date _____

Date of 2nd contact _____ Outcome _____

Follow-up date _____

Notes _____

_____

Mortgage Accounts

Debt priority # _____

Account Status
☐ Was late
☐ Is late
☐ Foreclosure filed

Account number _____

Lender name _____

Address _____

_____

Property Address _____

Phone # (___) _____ Section # _____ Block # _____ Lot # _____

Mortgage Value _____ Yearly taxes _____%

Balance $_____ Annual percentage rate _____%

Payment $_____ Total interest owed $_____

PAYMENT HISTORY

Month/Year of last payment _____

How many payments have you missed _____

Total amount overdue (update every 30 days) _____

CONTACTS FOR NEGOTIATION

First Contact Person

Name _____ Direct Phone (____) _____

Address _____

Date of 1st contact _____ Outcome _____

Follow-up date _____

Date of 2nd contact _____ Outcome _____

Follow-up date _____

Date notice of claim sent _____ Date federal suit filed _____

Second Contact Person

Name _____ Direct Phone (____) _____

Address _____

Date of 1st contact _____ Outcome _____

Follow-up date _____

Date of 2nd contact _____ Outcome _____

Follow-up date _____

Notes _____

Car Loans

Debt priority # _____

Account Status

☐ Was late

Account number _____

☐ Is late

Lender name _____

☐ Repossessed/Returned
   to owner

Address _____

☐ End of lease

_____

Phone # (___) _____   Equity (if any) _____

Balance $_____ Annual percentage rate_____% (Value—Balance Due)

Payment $_____ Total interest owed $_____

PAYMENT HISTORY

Month/Year of last payment _____

How many payments have you missed _____

Total amount overdue (update every 30 days) _____

CONTACTS FOR NEGOTIATION

First Contact Person

Name _____ Direct Phone (____) _____

Address _____

Date of 1st contact _____ Outcome _____

Follow-up date _____

Date of 2nd contact _____ Outcome _____

Follow-up date _____

Date notice of claim sent _____ Date federal suit filed _____

Second Contact Person

Name _____ Direct Phone (____) _____

Address _____

Date of 1st contact _____ Outcome _____

Follow-up date _____

Date of 2nd contact _____ Outcome _____

Follow-up date _____

Notes _____

_____

Bank Loans/Unsecured Loans

Debt priority # _____

Account Status

☐ Was late   ☐ Collections
☐ Is late   ☐ Judgment

Account number _____

Lender name _____

Address _____

_____

Phone # (___) _____

Balance $_____ Annual percentage rate _____%

Payment $_____ Total interest owed $_____

PAYMENT HISTORY

Month/Year of last payment _____

How many payments have you missed _____

Total amount overdue (update every 30 days) _____

CONTACTS FOR NEGOTIATION

First Contact Person

Name _____ Direct Phone (____) _____

Address _____

Date of 1st contact _____ Outcome _____

Follow-up date _____

Date of 2nd contact _____ Outcome _____

Follow-up date _____

Date notice of claim sent _____ Date federal suit filed _____

Second Contact Person

Name _____ Direct Phone (____) _____

Address _____

Date of 1st contact _____ Outcome _____

Follow-up date _____

Date of 2nd contact _____ Outcome _____

Follow-up date _____

Notes _____

_____

Medical Account

Debt priority # _____

Account Status

☐ Was late ☐ Charge off
☐ Is late ☐ Judgment
☐ Collection

Account number _____

Doctor/Facility name _____

Address _____

_____

Phone # (___) _____

Balance $_____ Minimum payment $ _____%

Terms of Payment Agreement _____

PAYMENT HISTORY

Month/Year of last payment _____

How many payments have you missed _____

Total amount overdue (update every 30 days) _____

CONTACTS FOR NEGOTIATION

First Contact Person

Name _____ Direct Phone (____) _____

Address _____

Date of 1st contact _____ Outcome _____

Follow-up date _____

Date of 2nd contact _____ Outcome _____

Follow-up date _____

Date notice of claim sent _____ Date federal suit filed _____

Second Contact Person

Name _____ Direct Phone (____) _____

Address _____

Date of 1st contact _____ Outcome _____

Follow-up date _____

Date of 2nd contact _____ Outcome _____

Follow-up date _____

Notes _____

_____

Student Loans

Debt priority # _____

Account Status

- ☐ Was late   ☐ Default/
- ☐ Is late   Government
- ☐ Collection   guarantee
                         executed
                     ☐ Judgment

Account number _____

Lender name _____

Address _____

_____

Balance $_____ Annual percentage rate_____%

Minimum payment $_____ Total interest owed $_____

PAYMENT HISTORY

Month/Year of last payment _____

How many payments have you missed _____

Total amount overdue (update every 30 days) _____

CONTACTS FOR NEGOTIATION

First Contact Person

Name _____ Direct Phone (____) _____

Address _____

Date of 1st contact _____ Outcome _____

Follow-up date _____

Date of 2nd contact _____ Outcome _____

Follow-up date _____

Date notice of claim sent _____ Date federal suit filed _____

Second Contact Person

Name _____ Direct Phone (____) _____

Address _____

Date of 1st contact _____ Outcome _____

Follow-up date _____

Date of 2nd contact _____ Outcome _____

Follow-up date _____

Notes _____

_____

IRS Settlements/Tax Debts

Debt priority # _____

Account Status
☐ Settlement agreement
☐ Installation agreement
☐ Collection
☐ Tax lien

Account number _____

Lender name _____

Address _____

_____

Phone # (___) _____

Balance $_____ Annual percentage rate_____%

Minimum payment $_____ Total interest owed $_____

PAYMENT HISTORY

Month/Year of last payment _____

How many payments have you missed _____

Total amount overdue (update every 30 days) _____

CONTACTS FOR NEGOTIATION

First Contact Person

Name _____ Direct Phone (____) _____

Address _____

Date of 1st contact _____ Outcome _____

Follow-up date _____

Date of 2nd contact _____ Outcome _____

Follow-up date _____

Date notice of claim sent _____ Date federal suit filed _____

Second Contact Person

Name _____ Direct Phone (____) _____

Address _____

Date of 1st contact _____ Outcome _____

Follow-up date _____

Date of 2nd contact _____ Outcome _____

Follow-up date _____

Notes _____

_____

FINANCIAL SUMMARY STATEMENT

Now that you have completed the account form or forms, your next step is to create a financial summary statement—a picture of your personal finances that includes the following:

1. Total debt
2. Total monthly minimum debt payment, including personal expenses
3. Total income
4. Assets
5. Discretionary income: total income minus the total monthly minimum debt and minimum personal expenses

The information you compile here is similar to forms completed when you originally applied for credit. This form, however, is your private information. When you begin a settlement process, creditors may want to know about your assets with an eye toward liquidation or seizure. Just because you've recorded them here doesn't mean you should freely disclose them during your negotiations, though the topic may come up.

Your income, debts, and assets are listed on your financial summary form to create a complete picture of your resources and liabilities. You'll probably want to avoid liquidating assets, but they need to be part of your decision process when considering how to settle your debts. Though liquidation is admittedly a radical solution, excellent credit can positively affect your finances to such a great extent that temporarily liquidating assets can actually pay in the end. For example, if you sell an asset and use that money to pay off a number of debts, fixing your credit in the process, your improved standing might get you a mortgage loan at a more favorable rate, saving you thousands of dollars. (See chart on page 54, A versus B Credit.)

Your income as stated on this form should include all your available money sources. This is different from a credit application, which may be limited to your personal income. There may be other resources you can tap into: your spouse's income or one-time payments that aren't part of your regular earnings, for example. These may enter into your calculation on debt settlement.

Using the account summary forms you've recently completed, along with copies of your pay stubs, tax forms, and/or other income documents, you should now fill out the Personal Financial Statement. Remember to work in light pencil, or photocopy the form, so you can erase and reenter figures as your situation changes over time.

PERSONAL FINANCIAL STATEMENT

Liabilities

mortgages, auto loans, credit cards, cost of living

Name of Creditor/Expense	A-Total Amount Owed	B-Minimum Monthly Payment	C-Total Back Payments
1			
2			
3			
4			
5			
6			
7			
8			
9			

Total of Column A = Your Total Debts $ _____

Total of B = Your Monthly Fixed Debt $ _____

Total of C = Your Back Payments Due to Lenders $ _____

Income

salary, rental income, investments (stock dividends), other

Source of Income	A-Weekly Amount	B-Monthly Amount	C-Yearly Amount
1			
2			
3			
4			
5			

Total of A = Your Weekly Available Income $ _____

Total of B = Your Monthly Available Income $ _____

Total of C = Your Yearly Available Income $ _____

Assets

cash on hand, jewelry, art, real estate, stock, CDs, other

Name of Asset	A-Value of Asset	B-Amount Owed	C-Could Be Liquidated Y/N
1			
2			
3			
4			
5			
6			
7			
8			
9			

Total of A = Total Gross Value $ _____

Total of B = Total Debt $ _____

Subtract B from A = Total Net Worth $ _____

Use the space below to figure and record the fluctuations in your income, assets, and debts, and other notes that you'll want readily available as you negotiate. Your personal financial statement is the sum of all the work you've done so far. It gives you the perspective necessary to make detailed plans that you can stick to.

_____

_____

_____

_____

_____

_____

_____

_____

MAKING YOUR PRIORITY PLAN: SUGGESTED ORDER OF DEBT IMPORTANCE

The overall test we suggest in triaging your debt is to arrange your new payments with the minimum additional damage to your credit and lifestyle. The plan that best limits such damage differs for each individual. As you begin to assign a priority to paying your debts, remember that after reading the negotiation section and actually talking to your creditors, you may alter your original plan.

The following is a list of credit topics. Each topic is followed by a general payment priority number. The number represents a suggested order of consideration on which debt should be paid. We also labeled each topic with a credit repair difficulty level, ranging from easy to hard.

Mortgages

<u>Payment priority #1</u>
<u>Credit repair difficulty level:</u> Hard

If you've never been late on your mortgage, we don't recommend that you freeze or pay these debts late. If you are already late on a mortgage payment, but foreclosure hasn't begun, we also don't recommend that you incur any more late payments or go into deeper arrears. A good strategy is to take all your resources away from the other lender classes, except for auto loans, leases, and other secured loans, and devote them to your mortgage, since other lenders are more easily pushed into a compromise that involves a settlement with clear credit.

Mortgages are among the most difficult items to repair. It is sometimes possible to force an accounts history to be unrated as part of the settlement of a legal action you might bring using the forms in this book. Additionally, you can negotiate to surrender your deed in-lieu-of foreclosure. Though this is not great for your creditor, it is better than a foreclosure. The credit bureau dispute method can occasionally eliminate derogatory information on a past, paid mortgage, since this information is often archived and difficult to confirm in a timely manner as required by credit law. (See page 128.)

IRS

<u>PAYMENT PRIORITY #2</u>
<u>CREDIT REPAIR DIFFICULTY LEVEL</u>: Hard

The IRS should be considered next, because it can reach right into your bank account or contact your employer and grab your money, even take your house. By addressing the IRS directly, this won't happen, since it can't break any agreement it makes with you, and it won't grab your cash if you are paying. (See Chapter 9, "More Credit Topics.")

The IRS doesn't negotiate credit reporting. Still, this may not be a priority credit repair item, so long as the lien is paid, since many lenders realize the aggressive nature of the tax authorities, and having a paid tax lien on your report isn't entirely rare or of great consequence provided most other credit accounts are reported in a positive light.

Auto Lenders

<u>PAYMENT PRIORITY #3</u>
<u>CREDIT REPAIR DIFFICULTY LEVEL</u>: Hard

Getting to and from work is likely a high priority. Auto loans can be quite difficult to fix on your credit report. The major difference between your car and your home is that auto lenders don't want your car back. Its value drops dramatically from the moment you leave the lot, as opposed to your house and property, which are likely to increase in value over time. So long as you are making some payments, or negotiating to pay your auto lender, it is unlikely it will seize your car. Maintaining communication is key. On your account form, keep track of whom you speak to. A written record will help your case in any dispute.

If you are leasing a car, your chance of losing it to repossession is greater because the lender isn't receiving payments toward its value, just its use. With this greater exposure comes a quicker reflex to grab the car and try to salvage something. Once you do have late payments with an auto lender, it usually takes rather aggressive action to cause this credit area to be cleaned up.

You can reinstate your loan in many jurisdictions by repaying the back debt, but we recommend that you do only what you must to keep current with car payments. Selling the auto before repossession may be wise, but you must first clear the title with the lender/lien holder. If you sell the car for less than you owe, you must negotiate with the lender to make sure that they accept those terms. You may be responsible for the difference between the sale price and the amount owed on the loan. If you can't get what you owe on the car, you should still consider paying the deficiency and liquidating. On paid leases and auto loans, the credit bureau dispute method can be effective. (See page 128.)

Credit Cards

PAYMENT PRIORITY #4
CREDIT REPAIR DIFFICULTY LEVEL: Easier

You can live without them, but preserving at least one is a good idea. Credit card debt, since it is unsecured, offers a number of meaty opportunities for clean credit and settlement despite late payments or lack of payments. Banks, however, are quite regulated, and it takes specific terms and conditions for them to clear your debt and record. This is known as unrating an account, and techniques for achieving this are discussed in Chapter 5, "Negotiation."

Store Cards

PAYMENT PRIORITY #5
CREDIT REPAIR DIFFICULTY LEVEL: Easiest

Store cards, likely the least important creditors, are among the easiest to negotiate clear credit and settlement on since they are totally unsecured loans based on merchandise that was significantly marked up. A retail lender can often realize a profit even if it settles for less than 100 percent. Retail credit cards are also a different class of loan from bank cards, since retailers don't have to report to federal regulators about their settlement procedures and policies as banks do.

Call, offer to pay for clear credit, and settle using the letter on page 123.

ISSUES TO CONSIDER

Many creditors want to know your discretionary income so they can include this money in a repayment plan. Don't tell them. It's your business, not theirs. If you went to a credit counselor, he or she would also attempt to tap this entire figure, saying you owe the money and should put the creditors in first position in your payment priorities. The philosophy of this book is quite different. We believe that you have a right to live and that *you* should be in first place. If, after subtracting debts from income, the number is too small to live comfortably, then it's time to reduce the monthly minimums. Essentially, work backward. Decide what you need to live appropriately and come up with a monthly minimum payment total that works for you. Keep that number in mind while you negotiate. You'll then need to consider how to divide this total among your creditors and decide whom to begin working with first.

For example, if all you can pay is 80 percent of your minimum monthly payments, one plan would be to reduce your payments by 20 percent across all your accounts. On the other hand, you may want to stop paying one creditor completely to arrive at this 20 percent. Your choice of which creditor might be influenced by whether or not it has reported derogatory credit or has a security interest in your property arising from the debt. If it has burned you, it can wait. This is especially true if a debt has been written off as uncollectable. It will wait until you have settled with other creditors.

Your immediate needs may affect how you plan to settle. If you are applying for a mortgage, for example, and want to remove two derogatory accounts in order to qualify, then choosing the creditors you owe the least money to and offering to settle the entire debt in exchange for clear credit may be your first priority. Removing two accounts can mean the difference between "A" credit, that is, a loan at the most preferential rates, and "B" credit, which costs more in interest rates and usually comes with higher loan completion fees (see page 54). After achieving your initial credit goal, you can reorder you debt settlement list in an overall effort to improve your financial health.

Unsecured creditors are often the first to jump for any settlement that will get them paid. After dealing with secured creditors that can take what is yours, unsecured debts are the most likely targets for quickly improving your position.

Since you probably want to hold onto some credit lines, consider choosing one or two bank credit cards you want to retain and keep them from your settlement list. If, however, the credit on these cards is seriously delinquent, you may want to consider including them in your settlement plans, even if this temporarily leaves you without plastic. After you've finished your repair process, you can always open up a secured credit card account, which makes sense for a number of reasons, not the least of which is that you won't incur debt beyond your means after you've worked so hard for your future. Contact the authors (see Authors' Services pages 4–6) for more information on obtaining a secured card account.

Since simply beginning a negotiation can stir some creditors to reevaluate your account, it may not be wise to begin discussion with those you can't afford to settle with. Some creditors, like the IRS, can't be unavoided. So it is a combination of your ability to pay, your decision on which credit you want to maintain, and your need to stave off serious actions against you that combine when you plan where to begin.

5.

CREDIT NEGOTIATION

—

 NEGOTIATE: *To carry on business, to confer with another so as to arrive at a settlement of some matter; to get through, around, or over successfully; to bring about a treaty, the act of or art of negotiating.*

Now that you've developed an initial picture of how to prioritize your debts, it's time to start negotiating with your creditors. In this chapter we give you a number of ideas and examples on negotiation. The goal is to contact your creditors and negotiate new agreements that make sense for you. The keys to success are being organized and detail oriented, and to negotiate from a position of strength. Don't be afraid just to dive in and try your hand at negotiating. If you don't have your act together on the first attempt, you can always wait a few days and you'll likely have a new contact to deal with.

AN EVOLVING PROCESS

Along the way to making your plans, you may decide to reorder your priority list; some creditors may settle immediately, while others may not budge an inch. If you decide to change your priorities, the forms on which you first established your plan can be altered. Since you may have more than one creditor and may have more than one contact for each credit account, always keep a written record of your progress on your account form's negotiation section. If you've already been contacted by creditors, you should record this information now.

Some accounts may not be susceptible to negotiation. You can use the credit bureau dispute method (pages 127–28) to attempt to repair where negotiation is fruitless or impossible. Again, some debts, such as repossessions and foreclosures, are quite difficult to remove by any method, though credit bureau disputes are worth a try, followed by a legal dispute should one be available. If all else fails, they'll come off your report in seven years. You will, however, need to verify that this happens, possibly prompting it by writing to the credit bureaus.

UNRATED CREDIT ACCOUNTS

Whatever your present credit report says is a matter of history and record. The large credit bureaus, like Experian, take the position that an account that has lots of late payments on it or has been written off by the creditor as uncollectable can't suddenly be made into an account that says "paid on time." Also, a bank, for example, can't lie. The very nature of its business is being honest, correct, and above suspicion. So what can it say about your bad credit to make it better? It can say *nothing*.

That's what *unrated* means. An unrated account is neither good nor bad and does not affect your credit rating. Accounts are often unrated because they are old or the information is suspect, or because you insist on this as part of the settlement terms in your negotiation.

Unrating an account in exchange for payment, or to settle a potential lawsuit, is the time-honored method of legal credit repair. We offer you both payment and legal process methods of accomplishing this goal. Money can lead creditors to unrate your account. Factually based legal argument can forcefully persuade them. If you've already paid the debt from which your bad credit arises, you may have only legal argument available. Don't worry. Legal force is an effective means of fixing credit. Your creditor is unlikely to spend more on a legal defense than you owe.

THE COLLECTION PROCESS

To understand the dynamics behind debt collection and, consequently, your role in this process, it helps to understand what actually happens when you become delinquent in paying your bills. At the time you become delinquent, a credit manager finds your name on a computer list of late payers who all share a common level of tardiness. This list is handed out to a number of euphemistically named *customer service representatives* (really, collection agents). At the early stages of lateness, the phone calls you receive from your helpful representative, in addition to the letter that is automatically generated, is basically a friendly prompt to pay. The collection process has begun.

The lender's collection techniques are part of a well-thought-out plan to manage an ongoing routine of getting money from customers, which after all is what lenders do. Some customers pay on time. Some pay when they are reminded. Some pay when threatened. Others pay when forced. Still others never pay. Each step along this chain is more costly in terms of correspondence and people time. It is important to understand that your position in this chain is only administratively distinct in the lender's eye—you are just a customer from whom money is to be collected. The lender will attempt to narrow the delinquent list by the path of least resistance. You can roll over and pay, or you can resist and negotiate for terms, in this case, an unrated account. Remember, only you can look out for your interests and make terms that fit your needs.

Your debt is currently at some stage in the collection process. By pushing for a negotiated settlement, you will likely wake up your lender and push the debt into the *recovery department*. Here, someone with true ability to negotiate new terms on your debt is easier to find. Unfortunately, some of the people who manage the interim stages of the collection process may not want to let you go easily, especially if their commission is at stake. They will tell you that what you want isn't possible. Still, it's important to go through the process of asking for a settlement, even if you have to repeat this as you climb through the levels of your creditor's organization. The following chart gives you a picture of the collection process.

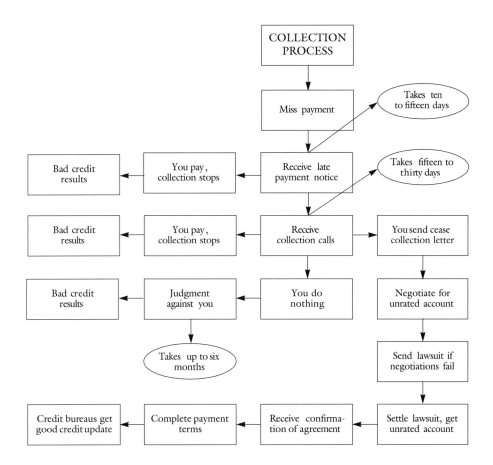

BUYING TIME

If you don't have enough money to pay your debts, or can cover only a portion of your minimum monthly payments, you may want to stall the process while you regroup and begin to work through your priority list. There are a few methods available to all consumers to slow collections while maintaining your present credit rating.

Revolving Credit

A bank credit card like Visa or MasterCard is considered to be revolving credit because the amount you owe and pay can change from month to month. The revolving amounts of lending and paying open these accounts to the possibility of error. The law recognizes this issue and affords consumers the right to have any potential discrepancies clarified and errors investigated. During the investigation, lenders must allow you all the rights offered in your initial credit agreement and cannot report any adverse credit. In fact, you have as long to pay as the lender takes to investigate and respond.

These rights are detailed in the Fair Credit Billing Act (FCBA). The act says that any item on a bill that you ask to be clarified through documentary evidence is technically a billing error. Until such time as your billing clarification request is honored, your creditor may not report the item as delinquent. (See page 121 for correction of billing error letter.)

IMPORTANT QUESTIONS

Using your account summary forms you filled out in Chapter 4, you can begin your negotiation with the first creditor on your list. No matter whom you start with, there are some basic questions you have to cover. As you go through this process, you'll begin to recognize common questions and answers in your exchanges with creditors. Through repetition, you'll become more skillful. The following questions are the basis from which you can develop your own negotiating style.

I'm calling to make arrangements to pay account #x. What is my current balance, and what are the minimum payments you will accept?

Creditors may ask why you need a payment plan, especially if you've been mostly on time to this point. If you are already delinquent, they may try for a full payment in a lump sum. This is part of their job, so don't be dismayed. They may initially offer you a payment plan that doesn't fit your budget, but you will arrive at a payment plan you can live with—they really don't have a choice.

If I can't make the minimum payment you are suggesting, are you open to an arrangement that actually fits my budget?

They'd better be. No matter what you hear at this point, stick to your guns and insist on getting a payment plan that fits your needs. If the person you are talking to isn't willing to make a deal, ask for someone who can. At the first level of debt management, the lowest-rung personnel will likely need permission from someone higher up actually to alter your original agreement. Once you have someone who can make a deal, insist on a payment plan that fits reality. For him or her to insist on anything else might cause you to look at bankruptcy as an option—say so. Also say that you have other accounts that agreed to cooperate and you need this creditor to be part of the entire picture or your plan may fail and no one will get paid.

Will you freeze the debt at its current amount (or the amount when it became delinquent)?

Often, a creditor will forgo interest payments and instead focus on getting the principal you owe. This is especially true with retail debts, where a profit was made on your purchase. Credit card companies that have collected high interest payments and are fearful of mounting defaults will also entertain freezing all interest payments, either from the day you start negotiating or from the month of your default.

Are you going to change the way you report my credit?

You need to clarify exactly how any payments will affect your past and future credit rating as part of any negotiated payment plan. Generally, if you are paying 100 percent of your debt, you can get an unrated agreement. Though it is possible to get unrated debt settlements of less than 100 percent, creditors are understandably resistant to leaving you intact if they aren't.

Will it show up as a settlement on my credit report or will you agree to *unrate* my account if I pay you as agreed?

You need the specific word *unrated* in any written agreement. You also need to keep any deal you make with the creditor. If you default anew on a renegotiated settlement, all bets are off. (See page 126 for an unrated agreement letter.)

Will our agreement be considered payment in full?

Be clear when you make your agreement over the phone. Even if you follow up, as we suggest, solidify your agreement in writing before you pay a nickel. Some unscrupulous collectors agree to anything you ask for to get your money, with no intention of keeping their end of the bargain.

Why won't you agree to unrate my account in exchange for payment? Haven't you done this for other customers?

The other side may tell you what you are asking for isn't possible. Rather than get angry, bring it back to the table. Everything is negotiable. Most creditors have agreed to unrated settlements in the past. Say that you know that unrated settlements are common, and if the person you are talking to can't make one, ask them to send you to someone who can. Though you may reach an unrated credit settlement, the odds are against your creditor showing you these cards in your first attempts at negotiating. This is especially true at the initial contacts with lower-level employees of a credit organization. They often read from a prepared script and simply don't have the authority to make these command decisions. It reflects poorly on them to fail in their collection effort.

Summary

The questions we suggest are geared toward pushing your creditors to a settlement. If they think they'll lose money by not dealing with you, they will be more eager to settle. Lending institutions lose money all the time and write off their losses. This is a last resort for everyone—it affects their profitability and it ruins your credit. By modeling the questions above, you can make a settlement that fits your budget and gets your creditor paid, leaving you with intact credit in the bargain. If you don't get what you want with your first negotiation, stick to your guns. As we've said, you will be tested. Remember, if you already have a number of late credit marks on your account, there is little more a creditor can do to ruin your credit. By holding out for your position, no matter how long it takes, you will likely get the settlement you desire. (To learn more about collection techniques, see Chapter 9, "More Credit Topics.")

CEASING PAYMENTS/COLLECTIONS

If you've decided not to pay certain creditors, or to hold off those that won't settle at this time, you want to stop them from attempting to collect the debt while you deal with your first priorities. This is done by sending a cease collection letter (page 117). Keep in mind that your debt will eventually reach the *recovery* department, the area of a lending organization most capable of making a deal with you. When this happens, you should begin making an agreement to pay and fix your credit. If you have never paid late and have perfect credit (though unlikely if you are reading this book), you should know that stalling your creditors with cease collection letters will add a number of derogatory late marks to your credit report and may cause the lender to seek a judgment against you. Carefully consider whether or not to settle unblemished accounts.

The goal of the debt reorganization process is to fulfill an agreement in which you demand from your creditors that they report your account as unrated in exchange for getting their money back. If, after attempting to negotiate with creditors, you don't think you can restructure your debt, bankruptcy may be your only choice. (See Chapter 6, "Alternatives to Credit Repair.")

JUDGMENT-PROOFING YOURSELF

You must answer any legal papers to hold off default judgments. If you take the route of ceasing all payments in an attempt to gain leverage in forcing a settlement, you expose yourself to creditor judgments against you. In the case of credit cards and loans, it is possible for the lender to gain a judgment against you within thirty days after you are mailed legal papers notifying you of your default and intent to seek court relief. If you don't answer, it wouldn't necessarily have to give you any additional notice of your court date, since your credit agreement and the law stipulate that it may seek a judgment after notifying you by mail and giving you reasonable time to cure your default.

If a lender does send you a summons and complaint stating its intention to seek judgment, you need to answer within thirty days. We suggest sending the appropriate summons and complaint form from this book before the lender begins this type of action so as to avoid being the defendant. By beginning the legal volley, you will likely push the matter to settlement long before its credit department comes after you. Still, if you are now in receipt of a lawsuit against you, it may be time to seek an attorney's advice. Though this costs money, it can save you from damaging credit that will be reported until seven years after you finally pay the judgment. If you feel up to it, you can negotiate directly with the collection attorney who sent you the notice and get his or her agreement to have the creditor accept payment in exchange for unrated credit. The attorney may not be willing, but if, with your own attorney's help, you answer the summons and complaint you've received, he or she is likely to become more pliable. No one wants to go to court. This is in keeping with our strategy of standing up for yourself and demanding, with force if necessary, that you get the terms you can live with. If facing off with an opposing attorney seems more than you can handle, contact the authors (see page 5) for referral to a competent attorney.

USING LEGAL MEANS TO FIX YOUR CREDIT

After you've exhausted your negotiation alternatives, you may have only legal means to convince your creditors to unrate your account. We are not suggesting that you sue if you don't have cause. We do believe, however, that a careful examination of the collection behavior of most creditors will reveal technical violations of the law. If your negotiation doesn't work, you should go to the questionnaires on pages 64–74, in which you'll fill out a detailed survey of your creditor's or collector's behavior. For the most part, answering yes to any question in this section means a creditor has violated your rights. If you believe that one of your rights has been violated, then you have grounds for suing. In our experience, the credit laws are sufficiently technical that most creditors and collectors have difficulty fully complying. Some of the questions you are asked in this section have to do entirely with your belief that something may have happened. If you believe something is truly a violation of your rights and the law, you won't be sending your lawsuit in bad faith, the test the court uses for making a valid legal claim.

CREDIT BUREAU UPDATES

Once you have succeeded in getting your creditor to agree to unrate your account, you need to write the credit bureaus and ask that they update their information. If your agreement calls for unrating the account in exchange for payment, you have to pay the debt before asking for the update. Since your creditor has agreed to unrate the account in writing, the bureau will double-check with them, and then, having either failed to get an answer or received the information that the account is unrated, will delete or unrate the account. Either is acceptable. To notify the three credit bureaus, use the bureau update letter on page 118. Remember to send the letter certified return receipt requested, and to repeat this process after thirty days, adding a handwritten note to the effect that this is the second time you are sending your request. The bureau will respond with a copy of your report showing the changed credit information. If the item still appears as it used to, don't despair. Often it takes creditors a number of weeks to update their files. You might want to confirm with your creditor that it has indeed begun the update process, and then repeat your letter-writing campaign to the credit bureaus at the appropriate time.

EXAMPLES OF CREDIT SETTLEMENTS

1. Have your creditor freeze the debt where it is now, or where it was when you became delinquent. Many debts have heavy interest charges (over 18 percent in the case of some credit cards). Getting the creditor to suspend interest payments and consider all future payment against principal can place a previously onerous debt within reach of your payment capability, especially if it is paid over a series of months or years.
2. Offer to catch up on all arrears in exchange for a positive account status. Many retail creditors are savvy to this offer.
3. Offer 80 to 90 cents on the dollar in a lump sum in exchange for an unrated account. Depending on your situation, you could even offer 50 cents on the dollar and negotiate up from there. Hypothetically, if you were about to go bankrupt in the absence of this agreement, your unsecured creditors would agree to the settlement in order to get paid.

EXAMPLE OF THE CREDIT REPAIR PROCESSES

Roy and Laura Davis wanted to get a mortgage, and at the best possible interest rate. Though they each had more than ten accounts reported by credit bureaus, with mostly good credit, each also had four bad credit marks. Consequently, most lenders would offer them only what's known as "B" credit—generally a couple of interest percentage points or so more than "A" credit. Over the life of a mortgage loan, these extra percentage points add up to thousands of dollars, as you can see in the following table:

Interest Rate (%)		Loan Amount	Total Interest on 30-Year Note
"B" credit	10.5	$100,000.00	$229,306.40
"A" credit	8.0	$100,000.00	$164,153.60
			$65,152.80 more interest

Roy and Laura's credit reports had the following negative items. We show the negative credit as it is reported by each bureau. The blank entries mean that an account is not reported by that particular bureau, not an uncommon occurrence.

Roy's report had the following negative accounts:

	Balance	TRW/Experian	Trans Union	Equifax
Visa	2067.00	Was 30, +2	47 0 0 2	(30)2 (60)0 (90)0
Macy's	865.00	Was 60	—	(30)0 (60)1 (90)0
IC System	239.00	Collection Account	—	—
GMAC	4300, 199/mth	Was 30	23 0 0 1	—

Laura shares some accounts with Roy, but not the GMAC car loan. She alone has a Strawberry's charge.

	Balance	TRW/Experian	Trans Union	Equifax
Visa	2067.00	Was 30, +2	47 0 0 2	(30)2 (60)0 (90)0
Macy's	865.00	Was 60	—	(30)0 (60)1 (90)0
IC System	239.00	Collection Account	—	—
Strawberry's	124.00	Was 30	14 0 0 1	(90)0 (30)1 (60)0

The Visa Negotiation

Using the format described in this chapter, Roy first called the bank that issued the Visa Card. His first contact in customer service told him that nothing could be done. It seems, however, that the Visa bill was paid late during the two months that Roy and Laura began their stay in a temporary apartment while trying to buy a home. Though they had made note of their move on a bill payment sent to the bank ten days before the end of the last billing period before their move, the bills were sent to their old address. Laura was organized enough to make a change of mailing address request with the post office, but that took a few weeks to take effect. Confusing the issue more, the person living in their old apartment continued to receive their mail instead of allowing it to be returned to the creditor.

Here's the point. You can preserve your billing address change rights only by making them in writing. The bank's representative asked, "Why didn't you call and let us know you'd moved?" That might have made things easier for the bank, but it's not what the law dictates. On the bill Roy and Laura sent in with their payment, their address change was correctly made. Unfortunately for all, the bank's automated system opens each payment envelope, searches for the magnetic stripe on the check, and throws the rest away. Their proper notice went in the garbage. By the time they finally got their bills after stopping off at the old apartment to pick up some boxes, they were sixty days late.

The bank's rep asked, "Didn't you know you owed some money?" That misses the issue. Credit cards are often referred to as *revolving credit* because the amount owed and the minimum payment due change on a month-to-month basis as you pay and borrow.

Simply put, you can't pay if you aren't properly billed. You have the right to receive bills at the correct address. If your written notice fails to gain you this change, you can't be marked late. After putting this argument in writing (see letter on page 121), Roy persuaded the bank to correct the credit. On the account form for credit cards supplied in this book, Roy recorded four different contacts as he worked his way up the chain of command to a bank employee who actually understood this aspect of credit law. Had his letter failed to get the proper result, he might have sent the Fair Billing Act summons and complaint to give notice of his potential claim in an effort to demonstrate how serious he was. If his notice did not generate appropriate action, he could have filed the complaint with the court. The letter notifying the bank of its billing error was enough, though. Most repair efforts end at the letter-writing stage.

The Macy's Negotiation

Department stores sell merchandise at a significant markup. Unlike a credit card balance that is profitable only when interest is paid, stores make a profit by selling you something. If you pay late, they add late fees. In the end, they want you to come back and buy more, even if you were delinquent in the past. Consequently, they are much more likely to forgive late payments in an effort to maintain good will. Though some stores are notable in their unbending credit-reporting policies, (Sears and JCPenney are examples), others have a cutoff limit below which they will remove the derogatory credit in exchange for your paying down your account to a zero balance. For Roy and Laura's sixty-day-late charge on their Macy's account, this was the case. A good rule of thumb in assessing credit-reporting leniency is to analyze the profitability of a creditor's sales. For instance, Sears sells home appliances with little markup and is quite tough about credit issues.

Laura called Macy's, asked what could be done, and was told that by paying the account off, her credit would be cleared. If the account had been more seriously delinquent, the store might have been less forgiving. Essentially, the policy of repairing credit for mostly on-time customers does not extend to records with charge-offs or collection accounts. Even ninety-day accounts might not fall into the "one-time courtesy" category, the phrase retail stores use when fixing credit. In the case of these later marks, negotiating payment for an unrated account is likely the best way to go.

The IC System Negotiation

IC is among the larger collection agencies, reportedly making more than 400,000 collection calls per day. The bill they contacted Roy about concerned laboratory work for dental surgery he'd undergone. Though his insurance paid the dentist, he mistakenly assumed that the lab work was covered in the dentist's bill.

After contacting IC, Roy discovered that he did indeed owe the money to a company called Western Labs. He checked his records and saw that the Western bill wasn't there. A quick call to Western confirmed that he owed $44.30. He was willing to pay, but he wanted to have the bad credit record removed from his file as part of the payment agreement.

Western was agreeable, but IC was another story. If Roy paid Western directly, IC would no longer be able to collect, and would not receive a commission. Also, IC depends on using bad credit to enforce payment on collection accounts. It knows that a collection account may eventually stand in the way of getting other loans, and consumers will eventually face this issue and pay up. Consequently, it doesn't take removing bad credit lightly—it's an integral part of its business.

Roy asked IC if it would consider removing the account if Western was agreeable, and IC said no. IC maintained that it reported historical facts—a collection account existed—and that to alter these facts would be lying. Even when Western agreed to ask IC to remove the item upon payment, IC resisted.

Roy first wrote IC a letter stating that the account in question had never been properly billed to him and was therefore unfairly placed in collection. He added that IC's continued refusal to look at the underlying facts in an effort to maintain its ability to make money was a conflict of interest.

With a copy of summons and complaint 2 (see page 93) concerning the Fair Debt Collection Practices Act, Roy was finally able to persuade IC how serious he was. In fact, IC might have unknowingly violated a debt collection practices rule by continuing to try to collect after knowing that the debt was in dispute. Western was paid its $44.30, and after sending the credit bureau update notices, the item was removed.

Conclusion

The GMAC account remained at the end. As we've said, it can be difficult to repair late auto payments. Laura negotiated the Strawberry's account in the same manner as the Macy's account. Roy and Laura's overall credit was sufficiently improved to get an "A" loan. The whole process took about three weeks of negotiation and four more weeks to get the credit bureaus updated.

6.

ALTERNATIVES TO CREDIT REPAIR

——

CREDIT COUNSELING

Many individuals with credit problems seek relief through non-profit debt-counseling agencies that masquerade as consumer advocates, such as Consumer Credit Counseling or Budget and Credit Counseling. These counseling businesses are better described as creditor advocates. Essentially, they make a standard arrangement with the creditors to administer your payment of approximately 80 percent of your debt spread out over the time frame in which you are capable of making payments, often up to six years. Then they turn around to you and make the same deal, but for, say, 90 percent of the debt, pocketing the 10 percent difference. Ten percent of millions in debt means big money for the companies involved.

Under the promise of relief from the pressure of debt collectors and mounting interest, unwary consumers are steered into payment plans that can best be described as onerous. While these companies typically arrange the freezing of debts at their current level by halting any further interest payments, the 90 percent settlement is made without an agreement to delete derogatory credit at the end of the payment process. These companies also fail to tell you that they will be listed on your credit report as administering the restructuring and payment of your debt, which is a derogatory credit mark itself. Future creditors will view you as having needed your hand held and therefore not adult enough to be worthy of the most favorable credit terms.

Many consumer credit agencies greedily coerce debt-laden consumers into payment plans with the same rhetoric that collection agents use. Upon calling an agency, you'll generally be demeaned with questions such as, "When you borrowed the money, you knew you'd have to pay it back, didn't you?" Once in their clutches, the agency will give you a form on which you are expected to divulge your entire financial picture, and then they will structure a payment schedule that essentially sucks away your entire discretionary budget—all money above and beyond your immediate rent, electric, and food bills. You can forget about going on vacation for the duration of your payout. In the end, the ones who get the most out of your debt restructuring are the credit counselors and the creditors. TRW/Experian's credit report often lists Consumer Credit Counseling's 800 number. This should tell you whose side the counselor is on.

The nonprofit status of these agencies should not lull you into a sense of security about their motivations. One nonprofit consumer counselor we know of is technically not allowed to carry any extra funds on its books from fiscal year to fiscal year but was recently reported to have made a book profit of $3 million, which was carried forward by special dispensation from the government agency that regulates this area of banking. Debt repayment is a big business. Consequently, debt consolidators process as many warm bodies as possible. When implementing your payment plan, they have their interests in mind.

The question then arises: If outside help isn't your best choice in correcting your debt and credit situation, what should you do? The answer: Do it yourself.

UNDERSTANDING BANKRUPTCY

When most consumers contemplate bankruptcy, they think of Chapter 13, especially if they want to save their homes. Chapter 13 of the Bankruptcy Code (11 U.S.C. Sections 1301–1330) lets you adjust your debts and make them more easily paid over time without the fear of having judgments and debt collection activity constantly badgering your every move. Chapter 13 is different from Chapter 7, because a 7 bankruptcy involves a liquidation of all nonexempt assets in return for discharging of all your debts. Chapter 13 allows you to keep assets and have a more complete discharge of your debts in return for agreeing to a payment plan based on future income. An advantage of Chapter 13 is that you can get a relatively speedy submission and confirmation of a payment plan. A disadvantage of Chapter 13 is that, unlike other bankruptcy forms, you have to pay money in the future, as opposed to Chapter 7, where you stop where you stand—liquidation is reached and you pay no further.

Chapter 13 is limited to individuals with unsecured debts of less than $250,000, and secured debts such as mortgages of less than $750,000. When you begin a Chapter 13 reorganization, you are protected by the court from any further collection efforts by creditors. Remember, though, that under the Fair Debt Collection Practices Act, you could write your creditors and tell them to no longer contact you, and they would have the option only of pursuing you in court. Under 13, they wouldn't have the court option.

Chapter 13 causes the creation of a *bankruptcy estate* in which all your assets are compiled. Unlike Chapter 7 liquidation, 13 is a reorganization. You continue to pay off debts, usually at some reduced amount, until the bankruptcy plan is finally discharged. This encourages individuals to try to make a plan for dealing with their debts, increases total payback to creditors, and should also be a hint to you of how the system works. Unless you have your back to the wall and are about to lose everything, making your own reorganization with creditors is likely your best bet.

If you do decide on Chapter 13, then a *trustee* is appointed by the United States trustee, a part of the court. There are no creditors' committees to review or administer the reorganization plan. If your Chapter 13 plan proposes to pay unsecured creditors less than 100 percent, the trustee's commission generally comes from the unsecured creditor's share of the debt. If you're paying 100 percent, then it comes from you. Since you will likely want to administer your plan to save money, this is a good reason to avoid 13 and make the deals on your own outside of the court system.

Essentially, the great allure of Chapter 13 is that it provides a broad discharge if the confirmed plan is completely performed. This discharge, along with your getting the opportunity to deal with mortgage defaults and save your home and other property, is one of the reasons to pick a 13 bankruptcy as opposed to a chapter 7 liquidation. Remember, though, that 13 stays on your credit for ten years and so should be avoided if you have any other options. Simply having late mortgage payments, though they stick around on credit reports for seven years, may not be reason enough to seek court relief. Making all your payments on time for a two-year period, in combination with clearing up all the bank credit card and retail credit card debts, will yield a significantly improved credit report and ability to get loans.

Among the items that a Chapter 13 cannot get rid of are student loans and liability arising from an automobile accident where drugs or alcohol were involved. Taxes are also covered in bankruptcy cases. Chapter 13 requires that taxes be paid during the life of the repayment plan, but it gets rid of all unfiled tax claims that are generally not discharged in a Chapter 7. It also eliminates a number of other debts and obligations that are covered in Chapter 7.

What Is Chapter 7 Bankruptcy?

Chapter 7 bankruptcy is a proceeding where all of your assets and debts (business and personal) are liquidated. The debtor (you) is required to turn over all nonexempt property to the bankruptcy trustee, who then converts it to cash for distribution to the creditors. You then receive a discharge, meaning a complete release from all dischargeable debts.

To use Chapter 7, you must be a United States citizen and have not used Chapter 7 within the last six years, or had a Chapter 13 bankruptcy. Also, you must not have had a bankruptcy filing invalidated by a judge within the last six months. You can't use the process to get better cash flow. It should be used only when your income won't cover your debts and expenses.

The following are items that can't be included in a Chapter 7:

- taxes
- spousal and child support
- debts arising out of willful and/or malicious misconduct
- liability for injury or death from driving while intoxicated
- nondischargeable debts from a prior bankruptcy
- student loans
- criminal fines, penalties, and forfeitures

Mortgaged or leased property may be included in a 7, but the creditor will likely take these secured properties back.

One benefit of filing a Chapter 7 is that most creditor actions such as debt collection and property foreclosure are stopped. Once a creditor or bill collector knows you are filing 7, it can't continue to collect. After your bankruptcy is filed, the court mails a notice to all the creditors listed in your filings. This takes a few weeks, though you can tell creditors of your bankruptcy filing and that will also stop collection.

Depending on how you file, you may exempt as much as $100,000 in equity from real estate. This value, based on a "forced liquidation," which is lower than the market value of the property, is used. Personal property such as automobiles, household furnishings, personal effects, jewelry, and work tools are also exempt. The value of each exemption depends on how you file bankruptcy. You'll need an attorney to guide you.

Alternatives to Bankruptcy

As we have said, it is probably in your best interest to work out your own deals with creditors. Bankruptcy should be a last resort. Even if your debts will take five years to pay off, this is still better than the ten years of bad credit that result from bankruptcy. When considering whether to file, judgments may be a pivotal issue. An unpaid judgment will stay on your report for the duration of the statute of limitations, twenty years. If you don't think you'll ever be able to pay it, it may be wise to consider bankruptcy. Also, if you are nearing the point where your creditors will seize your house, you may have no choice but to file. As we explained in Chapter 5, "Negotiation," it is possible to ask for reduced payments from creditors until you get your feet on the ground. Since your creditors may end up with only a fraction of what you owe in bankruptcy, they are likely to be open to whatever reasonable plan you suggest.

7.

THE LEGAL SECTION

 The forms in this chapter may be retyped with our permission, or they can be ordered directly from the authors, either as pre-printed forms with blanks for you to fill in, or on diskette as text files so you can alter them with any word-processing program. (See Authors' Services, pages 4–6.)

This chapter contains a set of *questionnaires* that enable you to decide whether your rights have been violated. After deciding which law(s) may have been broken with your yes answers, go to the *summons and complaint* section (pages 84–114) and choose the complaint that corresponds to your questionnaire answers. A *summons and complaint* is first used as a *notice of claim*. This means that you send it prior to actually filing with a federal court in an effort to inform the creditor/collector/credit bureau exactly what you think it has done wrong. If this does not bring the other side to the negotiation table, the summons and complaint section goes into the details of actually filing and conducting a lawsuit.

Chapter 8, "Letters," has all the necessary letters first to send your complaint as a notice of claim and then to send the same complaint after it has been filed through legal service. An additional set of documents, *a waiver of service* and *notice of lawsuit*, are included so that you can avoid the cost of service.

QUESTIONNAIRES

Here you will:

1. Answer simple yes or no questions about how a creditor or collection agent may have behaved.
2. Decide, based on your yes answers, which of the workbook's summons and complaints best apply to your case.
3. Prepare for a lawsuit.

Chapter 5, "Credit Negotiation," described the tactic of making a settlement offer coupled with demonstrating your capability of enforcing your legal rights. This approach sets you apart from most who argue for better credit. Though it may take a few contacts to convince the other side that you are serious, this method allows you to continue your quest for clean credit through a series of well-considered actions. Remember that lenders are in the business of loaning and collecting, not defending themselves.

The following questions, based on our understanding of the applicable credit laws, guide you in deciding if your legal rights have been violated. The questions are designed to let you choose either yes or no, with a yes answer indicating that a law may have been violated. Once you know which of your rights have been violated, you can choose the specific summons and complaint in this book that best fits your case.

Everyone should answer section 4 of Questionnaire 2, the Fair Credit Reporting Act questions (pages 73–74), since any credit problem generally will affect how your credit is reported.

Questionnaire 1
Fair Debt Collection

If the person who tries to collect a debt from you is not in complete compliance with a law called *the Fair Debt Collection Practices Act* (FDCPA), you can sue and receive money damages, possibly exceeding the amount you owe. We are not suggesting here that you sue anyone. You will, however, be in a stronger position to give a collection agent formal notice of a violation. If a collection agent realizes that you know your rights and can enforce them, the likelihood of getting him or her to delete a collection account from your report is much more likely. If you still owe on the debt in question, you may offer repayment as an additional inducement to clear your credit.

You don't need to be an expert or a lawyer—just answer these questions and we'll help you from there. The questionnaire is set up so that if you are able truthfully to answer yes to these questions (except question 1), then you likely have a case against the debt collector and could win money or at least present a creditor and collection agency good reason to settle a dispute. *This does not replace competent legal advice. Get a lawyer if you need one.* If you want to proceed on your own, we show you how.

If you can answer yes to any of the collection violations listed in the questions below, then use complaint 2, the Fair Debt Collection Practices Act and the Fair Credit Reporting Act summons and complaint (page 93).

1. Did someone who works for a company other than the company that loaned you money call you about collecting that money?

YES   NO

If you answered yes, then the law says this person is a "debt collector" and must follow all the rules of the FDCPA.

If you answered no, skip to Questionnaire 2, Fair Credit Billing Act (page 70).

2. Did the debt collector call anyone you know and ask about how to find your location?

YES   NO

If you answered yes, complete parts 2a–2g, below.

2a. Did the debt collector tell this person you know, without being specifically asked by that person, whom he or she works for?

YES   NO

2b. Did the debt collector call this person you know more than one time, without being specifically asked to call back?

YES   NO

2c. Did the debt collector mention to that person that you owe money?

YES   NO

2d. Did the debt collector ever send you or anyone you know a postcard?

YES   NO

2e. Did the debt collector ever send a letter that had information on the outside that would indicate that letter was meant to collect money (such as a return address of "Joe's Debt Collection Agency")?

YES   NO

2f. If you have told the debt collector that you have an attorney handling your case, has the debt collector still continued to call you?

YES   NO

2g. Has a debt collector called you before 8 o'clock in the morning or after 9 o'clock at night?

YES   NO

2h. Has a debt collector called you at work, after you have stated that this is neither convenient nor permitted by your employer?

YES   NO

3. The FDCPA allows you an important right. If you no longer want a debt collector to call you, by simply stating that you refuse to pay the debt or that you refuse to have further contact with the debt collector, he or she may no longer do so.

3a. Have you, your spouse, parent, or any other member of your household told a debt collector that you no longer want him or her to call or write?

YES   NO

If you answered yes, go to 3b.

If you answered no, go to pages 116–117 and copy the letter demanding that the debt collector stop contacting you.

3b. Has the collector contacted you again, either in writing or by mail, trying to collect the debt after being informed either by phone or mail that you do not want further contact?

YES   NO

After you have said in writing, "Don't contact me," the debt collector can send you one last letter to say that he or she may seek some specific remedy such as going to court, or even to tell you that he or she is in fact going to court. This is legal. But if he or she in any way tries to rehash the debt collection issue, this is not legal by our understanding of the law. Since this point is technical, we advise you to contact a lawyer if you have any doubts about the "final" contact after you have informed the collector to cease.

4. Debt collectors may not act in any harassing or abusive manner. Has a debt collector:

4a. threatened violence in an attempt to collect a debt?

YES   NO

4b. threatened to harm your reputation in an attempt to collect a debt?

YES   NO

4c. threatened to harm property in an attempt to collect a debt?

YES   NO

4d. used obscene or abusive language while attempting to collect a debt?

YES   NO

4e. caused your telephone to ring, or repeatedly contacted you for the purpose of annoying or harassing you?

YES   NO

   5. Has a debt collector used false or misleading representations in attempting to collect a debt, specifically:

5a. falsely claiming to be affiliated in some way with the U.S. government or a state government?

YES   NO

5b. misrepresenting the character, amount, or legal status of a debt? For example, claiming that a debt is being processed by the court when it isn't, or stating that it is older, or of a higher amount, than it actually is.

YES   NO

5c. falsely representing or implying that an individual is an attorney or that a communication is from an attorney? Many attorneys who collect debts employ assistants who, in our belief, imply by omission that they are attorneys. Only through careful questioning do they admit that they themselves are not attorneys.

YES   NO

5d. threatening to seize property or garnishee wages when not really intending to do so? Even mentioning this as a potential threat is, in our minds, implying that he or she will. If this is not the usual course of action in such cases, it is a violation of the law.

YES   NO

5e. threatening to take any action that he or she can't take or doesn't actually intend to take? Collectors can be aggressive. Even hinting at taking unusual or highly punitive action is violation of the law.

YES   NO

5f. threatening that the transfer of a debt will have negative consequences such as loss of rights or legal defenses? Debt collectors make their money by collecting. If you issue them a cease collection letter, they can't earn it and might make some sort of threat that you'll have more trouble, possibly violating 5d and 5e in the process.

YES   NO

5g. failing to communicate to third parties that a debt is disputed? The law actually says that debt collectors may not communicate anything that is untrue or that they should know is untrue. For real-life purposes, they often fail to tell credit bureaus and creditors that you are disputing the debt while they attempt to reverse your stance and get money from you.

YES   NO

5h. simulating documents that look like they are from a court or some other official source?

YES   NO

5i. using any false means or representation in an attempt to collect a debt?

YES   NO

5j. using any name other than the debt collector's true company name? We are aware of collectors who falsely say they are from your original creditor.

YES   NO

Questionnaire 2
The Fair Credit Billing Act

If you can answer yes to any of the creditor violations in this section, then use complaint 4, the Fair Credit Billing Act and the Fair Credit Reporting Act summons and complaint (page 105).

The Fair Credit Billing Act specifies your rights concerning the correct accounting and billing of accounts such as credit cards where the amount you owe can vary on a regular basis. Your rights include disputing or asking for clarification of a credit statement and receiving a bill at the address you specify.

1. Have you, within sixty days of noticing a billing error, notified your creditor in writing at the address specified for disputes, stating your name and account number and that you think there is a billing error?

YES   NO

If you answered yes, continue.

If you answered no but suspect that you have been billed in error, send the billing errors letter (page 121) now.

2. Has your creditor failed to send a bill to the address you have requested?

YES   NO

If you have changed addresses and notified your creditor within ten days of the end of any billing cycle of your address change, and your creditor has failed to bill you at the new address, that failure means that you aren't late paying the bill. Often, a creditor will ask you why you haven't called to give your new address, but this is not what the law dictates. The address change request should be in writing. (*It should be noted that sending a letter in with your payment may result in an automatic check-sorting machine removing only the check and throwing away the letter and envelope. This may actually be to your advantage, since a creditor can't easily dispute your claim that you notified it of an address change. Your claim that you asked for an address change, that bills continued to be sent to the wrong address, and that you now want to pay the bill you are only recently aware of in exchange for clear credit, backed by a summons and complaint under the Fair Credit Reporting and Billing acts, will generally be heeded if you are persistent and get to the right-level employee.*)

3. Did an error occur on your bill from a creditor:
- because the amount on the bill was wrong?
- because the bill failed to reflect a credit you were due?
- because you received goods or services you either didn't order/accept or that weren't delivered according to agreement or on time?

YES   NO

3a. Have you disputed this bill within sixty days of any of the above errors, in writing, and failed to have your dispute answered by your creditor? If you dispute a bill for any of the preceding reasons, your creditor has two billing cycles or ninety days to investigate and either agree or disagree. Otherwise, it is a Fair Credit Billing violation.

YES   NO

4. If you followed the dispute procedure in 3a, did your creditor:

4a. restrict your use of the account in any way before answering your dispute?

4b. report negative credit on the disputed amount to any credit bureau?

4c. fail to note that the amount was in dispute in any billing statements prior to the resolution of your written dispute?

YES   NO

5. Did you move, ask for billing at a new address, and not receive it there?

YES   NO

Questionnaire 3
Truth in Lending Act

The Truth in Lending Act (TILA) covers many aspects of *disclosure* in credit billing. The law is meant to protect consumers from many of the additional fees and points that crop up in loan/lease agreements. For the purpose of this book, the important question under TILA is:

In regard to an installment loan (auto loan, mortgage), did your creditor fail to clearly or meaningfully disclose:
  • **the interest being charged?**
  • **any finance charges?**
  • **the total amount?**
  • **escrow fees?**
  • **notarization fees?**
  • **appraisal fees?**
  • **credit report fees?**

YES   NO

Questionnaire 4
The Fair Credit Reporting Act

Under the Fair Credit Reporting Act, credit bureaus must accurately report information they supply to third-party lenders. Though some of the items we ask about in this section are straight out of the legislation enacted by Congress, other issues are derived from cases in which the law was interpreted by a federal court. An example of this is found in our first question. One case was interpreted by the federal court to say that credit bureaus have an obligation to investigate the underlying circumstances behind the credit they report. This means they can't freely report things if they have any reason to believe that they are wrong, and if they are so informed and continue to report, they can be held liable for damages.

1. Has a credit bureau reported information on your report that you believe is wrong?

YES   NO

2. Have you written to a credit bureau asking that it investigate the underlying circumstances behind a credit problem, and has it failed to investigate or correct the error within forty-five days?

YES   NO

3. Do you believe that a credit bureau that issued a copy of your credit history to a third party did not maintain reasonable procedures to ensure accuracy?

For example, if you applied for a mortgage, did another person's credit appear on your report because you share a similar name, or did the bureau continue to report an error even though both you and the creditor agreed that the bureau should change the item?

4. Do you believe that a credit bureau reported negative information on your credit even though the item was late as a result of incorrect billing or your not receiving a bill?

YES   NO

5. Did a credit bureau report negative credit on an item more than seven years old, or on a bankruptcy that occurred more than ten years ago?

YES   NO

6. Did a credit bureau report negative credit on your report that was not yours or was not your responsibility (for example, you were given a card by someone on his or her account, and that person had bad credit, and you never signed any agreement with the creditor)?

7. Did a credit bureau fail to respond to your written request for an investigation on a negative credit item?

YES   NO

Having gone through all the questionnaires, you should make a note of the questionnaires in which you answered yes to any of the questions. Remember that many of the issues covered deal with your belief that something was true. For example, if you believe that a creditor or credit bureau doesn't have suitable systems in place to avoid an error that occurred on your report, that belief alone may be enough to proceed with issuing a summons and complaint form.

HOW THE LEGAL PROCESS WORKS

At this point, you have answered questions to determine whether your rights under various credit laws may have been violated. These laws were instituted because of the uneven balance of power between consumers and creditors/ credit reporters. Not only has Congress recognized that the consumer needs protection, but the courts have increasingly become pro-consumer, if only in a cautious, plodding manner.

Making a Federal Case

This book deals with federal, as opposed to state, laws. Though you may pursue the rights these laws give in either state or federal court, here we assume that you'll go to federal court, especially because federal laws are the same in every state. Also, should you need to file your case, it can be done in any federal court in whose district either you or your opponent lives or does business.

Lawsuits brought under these laws are strictly governed nationwide by the Federal Rules of Civil Procedure (FCRP). You must follow these rules to correctly file a lawsuit.

So what does it really mean to start a lawsuit? When you sue, you bring your version of a controversy to the attention of the court. Under the laws we're talking about here, you are alerting the court to a dispute you believe exists concerning interpretation of the United States Constitution, because all federal laws are derived from this source. Sound serious? It is.

Article 5 of the Constitution prohibits the deprivation of life, liberty, or property without *due process* of law. *Due process* refers to the legal processes or procedures due to the participants in a legal dispute. The participants are often referred to as *litigants* or *the parties to the suit*. When you sue in a civil case, that is, a case between individuals, you demand that something be done to correct a wrong and/or that you be compensated for that wrong. Suing someone or someone's corporation and/or any other business entity for damages means that you intend to deprive it of money, which is its property. So anyone defending himself or herself from your lawsuit is due certain protections under the Constitution. These protections include the right to confront you, the accuser, in a court of law. He or she may also cross-examine you, meaning ask you questions to expose anything you know or believe within limitations set by the court. He or she can assert *counterclaims* against you: Specifically, he or she can add to the case you have started any claims he or she may have against you, even if it isn't a part of the original controversy, or he or she can do nothing—though that wouldn't be smart.

Some Legal Terms to Know

Before we get too far into the details and procedures, let's review some terminology you'll be exposed to when you sue. Over time, words and phrases that mean specific things in law have dripped down into common usage, diluting their original meanings. A judge, jury, or adversary will understand something quite particular, though, when you use these terms in their legal context.

If we follow the course of a lawsuit, also known as a civil action, many of the terms you need to know will arise. The action is commenced by *filing a complaint* with the court. The *complaint* is your statement of what is wrong, written in language acceptable to the court. In filing your complaint, you must follow the specific rules outlined in the *Federal Rules of Civil Procedure* (FCRP) or the result will be as if you did nothing at all.

Remember, the complaint asks only for help from the court in resolving your grievances against a third party—the *defendant*, so named because he or she must defend himself or herself from your charges. Because you are complaining, you are known as the [com]*plaintiff.*

Generally, a complaint is accompanied on a single legal document by a *summons,* which is provided by the court clerk. After filing with the court, you supply the defendant with a copy of the entire *summons and complaint,* the summons part summoning him or her to address your complaint's charges. The defendant's response is appropriately referred to as an *answer.*

According to the FCRP, the summons and complaint must be *served* on the defendant by someone uninvolved with your lawsuit who is at least eighteen years old. There is an entire industry of *process servers* who fulfill this task for a reasonable fee. A United States marshall or deputy marshall will also do, and if the defendant is a corporation, service can be executed by asking the secretary of state in the state in which the defendant maintains a principal place of business. Finally, you can mail a copy through the United States Postal Service, or by any number of overnight delivery services that make and keep a record of who received the document.

Another method of having the defendant served is to send a *waiver of service of summons* (page 112). This document is sent to the defendant in your lawsuit along with your summons and complaint. As the waiver says, parties to a lawsuit have an obligation to avoid unnecessary costs. If, after you send the complaint and waiver, the defendant does not comply with your request to acknowledge service, then he or she will have to pay the cost of service as described.

By following the above procedure, you *place a matter in issue,* meaning you make it the business of the court. In doing so, you also make a *claim for relief,* which is a request that you be compensated by the defendant, either with money, an affirmative act like correcting your credit report, or a negative act like never bothering you again.

If the person you sue answers, he or she *joins the issue.* Once issue is joined, the case proceeds through the court to a *disposition,* which can be either a *determination*—something about the case is decided by the court—or a *dismissal,* which removes the case from further consideration. Your case would no longer be on the *docket,* an official list of cases before the court. Yet another disposition is a *discontinuance,* which occurs most often when the parties in the lawsuit agree, or *stipulate,* that the court may dispose of the issue.

If the other party to your lawsuit does not answer within the time limits set by the court or FRCP, he or she is said to have *defaulted.* This means that he or she loses the right to defend himself or herself, and you have the right to a *default judgment.* This is different from a regular judgment handed down by a *jury verdict,* a decision made by a group of individuals chosen to listen to the evidence and make a decision on the case. Juries determine *matters of fact*— what actually happened. Judges determine *matters of law*—which laws apply to the facts, and how. Determining matters of fact and law are the only two things that occur during a *trial* of the issue.

You may know all the particulars about your case, and it all may seem very open and shut to you, but when you step into the world of litigation, nothing can be taken for granted. You must tell your entire story on paper, answering the classic questions: who, what when, where, and how.

You may think the incorrect credit report you hold in your hand is obviously flawed based on the facts, but the court will not share your opinion unless you prove it in a manner dictated by the court's rules. Actually, your complaint contains no facts, merely *allegations*—things you claim are true. Allegations that a judge determines to be supported by credible, relevant, and material evidence, or *proof* (determined to be so by a judge) will be submitted to a jury for *deliberation.* The jury will then determine which allegations are indeed facts. When the jury has determined the facts, it will then apply the law that has been given, or *charged,* to them by the judge. At the end of the jury's deliberations, it will make its *findings* and render a *verdict*—the jury's decision. The verdict is *entered* into the docket and becomes a *judgment,* which will remain enforceable for twenty years, or until satisfied by the losing party. *Note:* You don't have to have a jury to accomplish the jury's work. If you elect, a judge can decide the case. If you do want a jury, you must demand one in your complaint.

When should you start a lawsuit? The *statute of limitations,* or time you have to begin your suit, runs for two years from the date when *liability arises,* which can mean either the date the defendants did you wrong, the date you learned about it, or the date you should have learned about it. "Should have" means that if you receive a copy of your credit report containing an error, you must not ignore it and hope it will go away. A few days after the report was mailed to you begins the two-year limitation on your filing against your opponent.

There are ways to extend, or *toll,* the statute. For example, if a defendant conceals his or her wrong from you, or it is unreasonable for you to have discovered the wrong until a certain time, or the wrongdoing is continuous, you may likely toll the statute of limitations. This is a tricky area of law. Lawyers get disbarred for failing to work adequately within the statutes, so a word to the wise is: Don't delay, and if you are unsure, consult a lawyer.

After you file your complaint, you must serve a copy to the defendant within 120 days and prove that you've done so to the court by filing an *affidavit of service*—written proof that you have served your opponent.

Using a Complaint to Define Your Dispute During Negotiations

The court system, though in theory disinterested in the matters before it, is sufficiently busy that it encourages the outside settlement of cases. Almost all civil cases are settled out of court. The system might fail if this weren't so, because it couldn't handle the volume. This is a central part of the strategy we propose for the use of a summons and complaint. By sending a letter demanding a debt settlement you can live with and the unrating of your account, coupled with a neat, word-processed complaint, you demonstrate your serious intent and capability of enforcing it. Since the courts have extremely restrictive rules on the method and accuracy of filing a complaint, sending such a document will more than adequately express your side of the argument. Once your creditor sees all the legalese, he or she might conclude that you have retained a lawyer, and that the lawyer believes you have a case. Even if the creditor doesn't conclude that, spelling out what he or she did wrong in language that has been accepted by the courts could give your creditor a reason to renew negotiations. He or she understands that the next step is actually to go to court. Even the most intransigent creditor will see that you are serious about settling the problem.

If you were to threaten suit unless your creditor settled—but you actually had no intention of filing suit—that might be illegal. But we propose you send the complaint as a method of providing notice of your potential claim—a vastly different intent from extorting settlement under the threat of suit. You are, in fact, doing your opponent the favor of letting him or her see your side of the argument by sending the suit. The criteria for legally filing a lawsuit are straightforward. You must have:

1. a reasonable belief in the existence of facts on which your claim is based;
2. a reasonable belief that under such facts the claim is valid; or
3. an attorney's advice saying you have a case.

A litigant can be sued for "malicious prosecution," meaning that you are bringing a case against your opponent solely for the sake of using legal pressure as a bargaining or harassment strategy, not because you believe an actual case exists. The questionnaire section of this book is designed to tell you whether there are facts on which you can base your belief that a valid case truly does exist. Never file a suit for the sake of extorting your opponent into agreement.

Our practical experience in credit repair has taught us that even the best-run lending institution is hard-pressed to comply fully with credit laws. Congress, in an effort to strengthen consumer rights, has recently passed a number of revisions and amplifications of the *Consumer Credit Protection Act,* the umbrella legal act covering the credit laws in this book. We conclude that it is entirely likely your creditor has in some way failed to comply fully with the law.

One explanation for this opinion is that credit law is difficult to understand. In fact, the credit law specialty practice has few recognized experts, though the authors have attorneys on staff with credit law specialty practices. We have consulted for many attorneys over the years on the fine print of law and its impact on the repair efforts of our mutual clients. If credit is so specialized that it is difficult for attorneys, just think how hard it is for a lender to teach all its employees the ins and outs of the law and how to adhere to it.

A combination of Byzantine credit law and overworked, underpaid creditor customer service staff is fertile ground for violating the rules. The law has been interpreted by federal courts to deal with this inherent difficulty, by ruling that so long as a creditor has "a preponderance of systems in place" to avoid errors, it isn't liable for any errors that slip through. This "preponderance" language, though seeming to protect your creditors, actually opens up the door to your belief that your creditor doesn't have adequate systems in place to avoid making errors. If you do file a lawsuit against a creditor, it will be up to a court finally to decide if your creditor has complied with the law. Until then, if you in any way doubt that the creditor is in compliance, then you essentially believe that it may truly be at fault, and you can bring a legal action in good faith—the litmus test by which our system judges whether your action is serious or frivolous. Remember, we aren't telling you to sue—only how to do so if you deem it necessary.

HOW TO FILE A COMPLAINT

Read this section before you attempt to decide if you are willing to go through all the rigors of a lawsuit, a process that could take years and many resources. No matter which credit law you are suing under, if you represent yourself without the aid of an attorney, we urge you to carefully read the laws that apply to your case. In the questionnaire section, each credit law is listed and followed by a set of questions. If you answered yes to any question, then read the law (in Chapter 10 of this book) under which that question was listed. The exact guidelines for filing a complaint are in this book, though *Federal Rules of Civil Procedure* is a more authoritative source. Also, you should visit the *pro se* office in your local federal court. *Pro se* is the legal term that indicates that you are representing yourself without an attorney, and federal courts will guide you through civil procedure through the *pro se* office. If anything written in this section confuses you, ask an attorney for advice.

The Procedure for Filing a Complaint in Federal Court

1. Prepare your complaint. By following the directions in this chapter, you can easily use the complaint forms to create a usable document.

2. Take it to court. Show your complaint to the pro se office. Say that you want to sue and ask what to do next. There are self-explanatory forms you will be required to fill out.

3. Go to the clerk's office. Fill out the *civil cover sheet*, an information form used by the court. You must do this in triplicate and sign each copy.

4. File your complaint. At the writing of this book, the cost is $120. The clerk will assign your case to a particular judge and give you an *index number*. This number will identify your case on your complaint and any other document, motion, or court action arising from your case. When your creditor sees that you have an index number on the complaint you have provided, it will know that you have indeed filed with the court.

5. Ask the clerk for as many summonses as there are defendants in your case, plus one extra for your records. You may, for example, list both your creditor and a credit bureau in your complaint, and you will need to serve each of these defendants. No matter how many summonses you need, the clerk will provide them.

6. Serve the summonses and complaints. (We described the rules for this on page 76.)

7. Get an answer. After being served, it is most likely that the defendant will answer your charges, or possibly make a *motion* about the case. An answer might refute your claims point by point. It might say that your case has not been brought to the correct type of court (i.e., federal, state, civil, or small claims court), and/or that it hasn't been made under the correct laws, and/or that it hasn't been filed in the correct location, also known as a *jurisdiction*. Instead of an answer, the defendant might make a motion to dismiss your case outright, meaning that it wants the judge not to deal with any issue you've raised but to reject the whole thing.

Since you are a *pro se* litigant, the court may take the attitude that you are operating from at least a slight disadvantage. Accordingly, it may give you latitude to learn the ropes as you go and may also listen to your plain English and interpret it into legalese. Since the judge is under an obligation to administer your case and ensure that each party gets due process of law, it is possible that you will be spared some of the wrangling that lawyers often go through. On the other hand, interpretation of due process is often a matter of discretion by the particular judge administering your case. You may not get even the slightest break and could be rudely awakened by the process, with your case thrown away because of technical flaws in your performance. After all, the judge has no obligation to serve as your attorney.

8. Enter the *discovery period*. This is a part of the case in which each side makes requests of the other for information and/or testimony as it prepares for trial. This process is based on the antiquated concept that all the participants are "gentlemen" who honestly seek the truth with the aid of the court. In practice, though, it can be a dirty business of making onerous requests for huge amounts of information in an effort to bury your opponent in expensive, time-consuming work. If you have gone this far, it is entirely likely that you need competent legal help. Either the other side believes that it can't comply with your terms, or it wants to bluff, hoping that you will reach this stage where novices are ineffective and, so weakened, will make bad choices, including a bad settlement. In any case, we can't in good faith recommend that a novice enter alone into the discovery phase of a court case. It can involve a number of highly esoteric legal maneuvers that can't be taught in this forum.

9. Go to trial. Again, few should attempt this without a lawyer for the reasons just stated. There is no law against trying your own case. Indeed, the Constitution protects everyone's right to do this.

10. Receive justice. Since we can assume that your creditor defendant is represented by lawyers, you may find yourself in a full-fledged legal battle. While it's true that writing, filing, and serving a complaint can facilitate a settlement where none was previously available, the stakes are high; if you don't settle, you have to proceed to trial or withdraw your complaint. If you do withdraw your complaint, you could be accused of not bringing a *good-faith* action and be liable for money damages, though this is unlikely and would have to be decided in court in a separate proceeding.

SUMMONS AND COMPLAINT FORMS

This section has forms useful in filing suit for violations of:

- The Fair Credit Reporting Act
- The Fair Debt Collection Practices Act
- The Fail Credit Billing Act
- The Truth in Lending Act

The summons and complaint forms provided here are taken from actual cases. They cover filing suit under the above acts. Each summons and complaint actually includes a claim under the Fair Credit Reporting Act, because it is nearly universally involved in any credit issue. Also, the FCRA provides the practical benefit of allowing you to file suit for unlimited money damage, whereas the other acts have rather stringent limits on the amount you can sue for, as you'll see below.

The following has been reprinted from *The Consumer Handbook to Credit Protection Laws*, published by the Board of Governors of the Federal Reserve. It details other areas of potential lawsuits against creditors/credit reporters that can aid in your forcing a settlement.

> You may also take legal action against a creditor. If you decide to bring a lawsuit, here are the penalties a creditor must pay if you win.
>
> **Truth in Lending** (TILA) and Consumer Leasing Acts. If any creditor fails to disclose information required under these Acts, or gives inaccurate information, or does not comply with the rules about credit cards or the right to cancel certain home-secured loans, you as an individual may sue for actual damages—any money loss you suffer. In addition, you can sue for twice the finance charge in the case of certain credit disclosures, or, if a lease is concerned, 25 percent of total monthly payments. In either case, the least the court may award you if you win is $100, and the most is $1,000. In any lawsuit that you win, you are entitled to reimbursement for court costs and attorney's fees.
>
> Class action suits are also permitted. A class action suit is one filed on behalf of a group of people with similar claims.
>
> **Fair Credit Billing Act** (FCBA). A creditor who breaks the rules for the correction of billing errors automatically loses the amount owed on the item in question and any finance charges on it, up to a combined total of $50—even if the bill was correct. You as an individual may also sue for actual damages plus twice the amount of any finance charges, but in any case not less than $100 nor more than $1,000. You are also entitled to court costs and attorney's fees in a successful lawsuit. Class action suits are also permitted.

Fair Credit Reporting Act. You may sue any credit reporting agency or creditor for breaking the rules about who may see your credit records or for not correcting errors in your file. Again, you are entitled to actual damages, plus punitive damages that the court may allow if the violation is proved to have been intentional. In any successful lawsuit, you will also be awarded court costs and attorney's fees. A person who obtains a credit report without proper authorization—or an employee of a credit-reporting agency who gives a credit report to unauthorized persons—may be fined up to $5,000 or imprisoned for one year, or both.

Based on your questionnaire answers, choose the appropriate summons and complaint from those that follow, copy it with our permission, and fill out the sections according to the instructions.

The Parts of a Complaint

Each of the four complaints that follow gives specific instructions about what to fill in that is unique to that complaint, but all of the complaints include the following sections:

The caption is the official title of the case you are bringing against the company or companies that you feel have violated your rights as you understand them, having answered the questionnaires in this book.

A. The top line identifies the court, in this case the United States District Court in your jurisdiction. You can find the District Court that has jurisdiction, that is, the power to rule on legal matters involving federal law (such as this lawsuit), by calling phone information and asking for the federal court general information number from the jurisdiction that you are planning to sue in.

Fill in the blanks on the second line of the complaint like the example below. Some federal courts have more than one district, so it is important to find out which district you are in.

Example:

UNITED STATES DISTRICT COURT
Southern DISTRICT OF New York

B. The next part you must fill in is the line above the word *Plaintiff.* Since you are complaining about a violation of the law, you are the plaintiff. Put your name on the line.

C. The person you are complaining against, who will have to defend himself or herself, is the *defendant*. Fill in that person's name on the line. If you are complaining against more than one company or person, list them all, each on a separate line, with one under the other.

IMPORTANT: You must name the defendant with complete accuracy. For example, if it is a company called Joe's Credit Bureau, Inc., and you put only Joe's Credit Bureau, or abbreviate the name as Joe's Cred. Bureau, this may not be sufficiently specific under the law, and the person you are trying to take to court can ignore this as if you never tried to sue him or her at all. Also, some businesses work under one name and are incorporated under another. You can find out by calling the secretary of state in your state and inquiring. For instance, Joe's Credit Bureau, Inc., may have filed a Doing Business As (D/B/A) form with the secretary of state if it wants to operate under a different name. In this instance, you would cite the company as Joe's Credit Bureau, Inc. D/B/A Joe's Credit. We are aware of more than a few instances of cases being dismissed due to a faulty complaint that didn't properly identify the defendant.

D. The term *pro se* means that you are representing yourself without any lawyer. If you later decide to use a lawyer, this line will be changed to reflect that. Below the *pro se* statement, it says that you are making this complaint *upon information and belief*. This is a legal term that identifies the fact that what you are swearing to in your complaint is based on the information and beliefs that you have at the time you are making the complaint. By telling the court this, it leaves room for you, upon learning or discovering more or different facts, to change your stance on some of the claims you are making in this document. It is a term of art in the world of legal pleading that may have lost some of its meaning because if you don't use it, you can still amplify and/or modify your position, but since it seems to have worked for so long and shows a familiarity with pleading (which some lawyers call an "art"), there is no reason to discard it.

E. The *jurisdiction* section states your reason why this case belongs in a federal court. The case you are making involves the alleged violation of a federal law, making this a *federal question*. You are also specifically stating the federal laws that you believe were violated. By citing a federal question, you are granted access to the court's resources.

F. Since you have chosen a specific federal court for this case, it is important that either you or one of the people you are suing—the parties—reside or do business in that district. Alternatively, you can sue in the district where the alleged violation of the law and your rights occurred. The law allows you to assume that a business entity resides in any location where that entity does business.

For convenience, try to pick the court that is closest to your official residence. You will have to go to the clerk of the court to file this case (pages 80–81). Again, you must be extremely accurate here. Some creditors have one address where they accept payments but list another on their bill that specifies where they want disputes sent. Unless you use the correct address, it will be as if you didn't file suit at all. Double-check by phone or mail where you should serve legal papers on any business named in this document.

G. *Allegations* are your charges of wrongdoing. It is not uncommon to allege all the possible wrongdoings specified in the body of law under which you are suing, as we have done in the complaint forms. The rules of court procedure don't allow you to raise claims that haven't been discussed in your filing unless you have an explanation on the late inclusion of such a claim that the court can accept. This approach of alleging all possible violations lets you have the most room to bring newly discovered issues to bear in your effort to prove the defendant's wrongdoing. In the interest of *judicial economy*, however, we suggest that you take a pencil and strike out the allegations in the complaint that have absolutely no application to your case. Though it may seem more appropriate to retype the entire complaint, omitting the allegations that don't apply, using the complaint forms presented in these pages, even with whole sections crossed out, is acceptable to the court and will save you a great deal of time.

H. *Claims for relief* are your exact explanations of how you've been hurt, followed by the manner in which you wish to be compensated for the wrongs done against you.

Complaint 1.
The Fair Credit Reporting Act

This summons and complaint makes allegation about wrongdoing concerning the Fair Credit Reporting Act. Note that it allows you to bring suit against more than one person. You could, for example, use this complaint against a credit bureau that reported error in your credit report and also against the creditor or potential creditor that either generated the error or refused you credit because of it.

- In section 9, fill in the approximate date when the credit-reporting problem occurred. If the problem is ongoing, then use the approximate date when you know it had begun, or the last time the problem happened (for example, the same error appeared on yet another copy of your credit report).
- In section 10, fill in the name(s) of any individual who heard, saw, or received the allegedly incorrect credit report information. The date refers to the date of your cover letter to the creditor/potential creditor/credit reporter in which you stated in plain English what you think it has done wrong, thereby incorporating this letter in your complaint by reference.

UNITED STATES DISTRICT COURT
_____ DISTRICT OF _____

Plaintiff

—against—

Defendant

COMPLAINT
PLAINTIFF DEMANDS
TRIAL BY JURY

Plaintiff, appearing PRO SE, hereby complains of the defendant(s) and alleges upon information and belief as follows:

Jurisdiction

1. These claims arise under Federal Question Jurisdiction, including but not limited to USC Title XV—Consumer Credit Protection Act, Subchapter, Sections 1681 et. seq.—The Fair Credit Reporting Act (FCRA or "Act"), USC Title XV Sections and the law of this State where I live and where defendant(s) does(do) business.

Parties

2. Plaintiff resides at

3. Defendant(s) is(are) a domestic corporation having its principal place of business at

---

Name   _Address_

Name   _Address_

ALLEGATIONS

4. Plaintiff is a consumer within the meaning and purview of the act.

5. Defendant(s) is(are) a consumer reporting agency within the meaning and purview of the Act.

6. Prior to date of defendants' actions from which these allegations arise, plaintiff

    had a good credit record

    had good standing in the community

    had a job

    etc.

7. Defendants, alone or in concert, joint venture, partnership and/or some other contractual arrangement, violated the Act as pled herein and as to be discovered, thus causing plaintiff special, general and punitive damages.

8. Defendants, alone or in concert, joint venture, partnership and/or some other contractual arrangement, were negligent, thus causing plaintiff damages.

9. Defendants, alone or in concert, joint venture, partnership and/or some other contractual arrangement, then illegally produced and disseminated incorrect information on or about_____, thus causing special, general and punitive damages.

10. Defendants, alone or in concert, joint venture, partnership and/or some other contractual or non-contractual arrangement rendered, obtained, and or published such information, and or performed its obligations in a willfully and criminally reckless, negligent and/or illegal fashion in violation of the Act and the laws of this State and of these United States, in inter alia, failing to use and/or maintain reasonable procedures designed to avoid violations of Section 605 of the Fair Credit Reporting Act and/or other laws; failing to evaluate and/or re-evaluate any and all information; failing to authenticate information; disseminating such information; intentionally deceiving plaintiff who justifiably relied upon defendants' promises to plaintiff's detriment and damage, acting with malice, acting with presumed malice; acting with intent; acting with implied intent; asserting, maintaining, publishing and otherwise communicating certain false information about plaintiff; willfully failing to verify the information before publishing it; warranting, guaranteeing, representing, publishing and otherwise communicating that certain false information about plaintiff was true; breaching their contract with plaintiff, making untrue written and/or oral statements defaming, maligning and/or in other ways misrepresenting plaintiff and/or plaintiff's financial ability, status, competence, creditworthiness and/or life, publishing and/or otherwise communicating such incorrect and defamatory writing to third parties, including but not limited to _____ violating the law as detailed on the letter dated _____, sent by plaintiff to defendant, annexed hereto and incorporated by reference; and others as discovery will show; failing to check the veracity and accuracy of the information published, wantonly, willfully, recklessly and intentionally failing to use reasonable care in the course of its business; violating, inter alia, the Fair Credit Reporting Act, Title 6, Section 607(b); failing to follow reasonable procedures to assure maximum possible accuracy of the information on plaintiff, and in so operating its business so as to cause the damages to plaintiff.

11. Defendants knew, or should have known, that the information rendered and/or obtained was false, inaccurate and/or in some way inappropriate and potentially damaging to plaintiff.

12. Notwithstanding this knowing falsity, defendants nonetheless continued to render disseminated, provided, made available or in some other way published such false information to third parties to plaintiff's detriment and damage laws.

13. Defendants knew or should have known that their acts and/or omissions were or could have been damaging to plaintiff. Notwithstanding this knowledge, defendants continued to act or failed to act in violation of the Act to plaintiff's detriment and damage.

14. As a result of the acts of defendants, plaintiff was caused to incur general and special damages.

15. Defendants' acts were so reckless, wanton, quasi-criminal and performed with such disregard for the rights of plaintiff that plaintiff demands PUNITIVE DAMAGES.

AS AND FOR A FIRST CLAIM FOR RELIEF UNDER THE ACT

16. Plaintiff repeats and realleges all previous paragraphs with the same force and effect as if the same were set forth more fully at length herein.

17. Defendants violated the Act as complained of herein and in other ways as discovery will show.

18. Such violation(s) caused plaintiff damages.

AS AND FOR A SECOND CLAIM FOR RELIEF IN LIBEL UNDER THE ACT

19. Plaintiff repeats and realleges all previous paragraphs with the same force and effect as if the same were set forth more fully at length herein.

20. As a result of defendants' actions, plaintiff has been libeled and sustained damages thereby.

AS AND FOR A THIRD CLAIM FOR RELIEF IN LIBEL PER SE

21. Plaintiff repeats and realleges all previous paragraphs with the same force and effect as if the same were set forth more fully at length herein.

22. As a result of defendants' acts, plaintiff has been libeled per se and sustained per se and punitive damages.

AS AND FOR A FOURTH CLAIM FOR RELIEF IN SLANDER

23. Plaintiff repeats and realleges all previous paragraphs with the same force and effect as if the same were set forth more fully at length herein.

24. As a result of defendants' acts, plaintiff has been slandered and sustained damages thereby.

AS AND FOR A FIFTH CLAIM FOR RELIEF IN SLANDER PER SE

25. Plaintiff repeats and realleges all previous paragraphs with the same force and effect as if the same were set forth more fully at length herein.

26. As a result of defendants' acts, plaintiff has been slandered and sustained per se and punitive damages thereby.

AS AND FOR A SIXTH CLAIM FOR RELIEF IN DEFAMATION

27. Plaintiff repeats and realleges all previous paragraphs with the same force and effect as if the same were set forth more fully at length herein.

28. As a result of defendants' actions, plaintiff has been defamed and sustained damages thereby.

AS AND FOR A SEVENTH CLAIM FOR RELIEF IN FRAUD

29. Plaintiff repeats and realleges all previous paragraphs with the same force and effect as if the same were set forth more fully at length herein.

30. Defendants represented to plaintiff that they would accurately compile, maintain and/or disseminate information.

31. Such representations were false.

32. Defendants made such representations recklessly and without regard to their truth; knew them to be false; and/or had no knowledge of the truth.

33. Plaintiff relied upon these representations.

34. Plaintiff acted with ordinary prudence in relying upon such representations.

35. Such false representations injured plaintiff.

AS AND FOR AN EIGHTH CLAIM FOR RELIEF IN INJURIOUS FALSEHOOD

36. Plaintiff repeats and realleges all previous paragraphs with the same force and effect as if the same were set forth more fully at length herein.

37. As a result of defendants' acts, plaintiff has been damaged as a result of defendants communicating injurious falsehoods.

AS AND FOR A NINTH CLAIM FOR RELIEF IN INTENTIONAL INFLICTION OF EMOTIONAL DISTRESS

38. Plaintiff repeats and realleges all previous paragraphs with the same force and effect as if the same were set forth more fully at length herein.

39. As a result of defendants' intentional acts, plaintiff has suffered and continues to suffer emotional distress and other diminishments of plaintiff's quality of life.

AS AND FOR A TENTH CLAIM FOR RELIEF IN NEGLIGENT INFLICTION OF EMOTIONAL DISTRESS

40. Plaintiff repeats and realleges all previous paragraphs with the same force and effect as if the same were set forth more fully at length herein.

41. As a result of defendants' negligent acts, plaintiff has suffered and continues to suffer emotional distress and other diminishments of the quality of plaintiff's life.

AS AND FOR AN ELEVENTH CLAIM FOR RELIEF FOR BREACH OF CONTRACT

42. Plaintiff repeats and realleges all previous paragraphs with the same force and effect as if the same were set forth more fully at length herein.

43. As a result of defendants' acts amounting to breach of contract, plaintiff has been damaged.

WHEREFORE, plaintiff demands judgment against defendants in a sum in excess of $50,000 (FIFTY THOUSAND DOLLARS) in the first claim for relief, in a sum in excess of $50,000 (FIFTY THOUSAND DOLLARS) in the second claim for relief, in a sum in excess of $50,000 (FIFTY THOUSAND DOLLARS) in the third claim for relief, in a sum in excess of $50,000 (FIFTY THOUSAND DOLLARS) in the fourth claim for relief, in a sum in excess of $50,000 (FIFTY THOUSAND DOLLARS) in the fifth claim for relief, in a sum in excess of $50,000 (FIFTY THOUSAND DOLLARS) in the sixth claim for relief, in a sum in excess of $50,000 (FIFTY THOUSAND DOLLARS) in the seventh claim for relief, in a sum in excess of $50,000 (FIFTY THOUSAND DOLLARS) in the eighth claim for relief, in the sum in excess of $50,000 (FIFTY THOUSAND DOLLARS) in the ninth claim for relief, in the sum in excess of $50,000 (FIFTY THOUSAND DOLLARS) in the tenth claim for relief, in the sum in excess of $50,000 (FIFTY THOUSAND DOLLARS) in the eleventh claim for relief; PUNITIVE DAMAGES FOR ALL CLAIMS AS SET BY THE JURY OR THE COURT, together with attorney's fees, the costs and disbursements of this action and such other relief this court may deem just and proper.

_____   _____
Signed   *Dated*

Complaint 2.
The Fair Debt Collection Practices Act and the Fair Credit Reporting Act

This summons and complaint makes allegations about wrongdoing concerning both the Fair Debt Collection Practices Act and the Fair Credit Reporting Act. It allows you to bring suit against more than one person. You could, for example, use this complaint against a collection agent who abused the collection process, a credit bureau that reported error in your credit report possibly resulting from the abusive collection, and a creditor that wrongly placed the account in collection.

- In section 9, fill in the approximate date when the collection violation occurred. If the problem is ongoing, then use the approximate date when you know it had begun, or the last time the problem happened (for example, the same company attempted to collect the debt by phone or mail on yet another occasion).
- In section 10, fill in the name of the person(s) who saw your report where indicated. The date refers to the date of your cover letter to the creditor/potential creditor/credit reporter in which you stated in plain English what you think it has done wrong, thereby incorporating this letter in your complaint by reference.

UNITED STATES DISTRICT COURT
_____ DISTRICT OF _____

<table>
<tr><td>

COMPLAINT
PLAINTIFF DEMANDS
TRIAL BY JURY
</td></tr>
</table>

_____
Plaintiff

   —against—

_____
Defendant

Plaintiff, appearing PRO SE, hereby complains of the defendant(s) and alleges upon information an belief as follows:

Jurisdiction

1. These claims arise under Federal Question Jurisdiction, including but not limited to USC Title VI—Consumer Credit Protection Act, Subchapter, Sections 1681 et. seq.—The Fair Credit Reporting Act (FCRA or "Act 1"), and Sections 1692 et. seq.—The Fair Debt Collection Practices Act (FDCPA or "Act 2"), (both acts hereinafter referred to collectively as the "Acts") and the law of this State where I live and where defendant(s) does(do) business.

Parties

2. Plaintiff resides at

3. Defendant(s) is(are) a domestic corporation having its principal place of business at

_____	_____
Name	*Address*
_____	_____
Name	*Address*

ALLEGATIONS

4. Plaintiff is a consumer within the meaning and purview of the Act.

5. Defendant(s) is(are) a debt collection agency within the meaning and purview of Act 2 or Defendant(s) is(are) a consumer reporting agency within the meaning and purview of Act 1.

6. Prior to date of defendants' actions from which these allegations arise, plaintiff

had a good credit record

had good standing in the community

had a job

etc.

7. Plaintiff was the subject of collection efforts and credit reporting concerning a debt, defined under the meaning and purview of Act 2.

8. Defendants, alone or in concert, joint venture, partnership and/or some other contractual arrangement, violated the Acts as pled herein and as to be discovered, thus causing plaintiff special, general and punitive damages.

9. Defendants, alone or in concert, joint venture, partnership and/or some other contractual arrangement, produced or created, or caused to be produced or created, disseminate or published, or caused to be disseminated or published, incorrect and false information pertaining to plaintiff on or about _____ to persons identified more fully herein, causing plaintiff damages.

10. Defendants, alone or in concert, joint venture, partnership and/or some other contractual arrangement rendered, obtained, and/or published such information, and/or performed its obligations in a willfully and criminally reckless, negligent and/or illegal fashion in violation of the Act and the laws of this State and of these United States, in inter alia, failing to use and/or maintain reasonable procedures designed to avoid violations of Section 605 of the Fair Credit Reporting Act and/or other laws; failing to evaluate and/or re-evaluate any and all information; failing to authenticate information; disseminating such information; intentionally deceiving plaintiff who justifiably relied upon defendants' promises to plaintiff's detriment and damage, acting with malice, acting with presumed malice; acting with intent; acting with implied intent; asserting, maintaining, publishing and otherwise communicating certain false information about plaintiff; willfully failing to verify the information before publishing it; warranting, guaranteeing, representing, publishing and otherwise communicating that certain false information about plaintiff was true; breaching their contract with plaintiff, making untrue written and/or oral statements defaming, maligning and/or in other ways misrepresenting plaintiff and/or plaintiff's financial ability, status, competence, creditworthiness and/or life, publishing and/or otherwise communicating such incorrect and defamatory writing to third parties, including but not limited to _____; violating the law as detailed on the letter dated _____, sent by plaintiff to defendant, annexed hereto and incorporated by reference; and others as discovery will show; failing to check the veracity and accuracy of the information published, wantonly, willfully, recklessly and intentionally failing to use reasonable care in the course of its business; violating, inter alia, the Fair Credit Reporting Act, Title 6, Section 607(b);

failing to follow reasonable procedures to assure maximum possible accuracy of the information on plaintiff, and in so operating its business so as to cause the damages to plaintiff.

AND

Defendants, alone or in concert, joint venture, partnership and/or some other contractual or non-contractual arrangement, in attempting to collect the debt described herein, used or attempted to use false, misleading, abusive, unfair and/or deceptive means, presentations and/or procedures, including but not limited to the following: failing to send verification of debt; failing to properly verify the debt; collecting an amount besides the debt to which defendants were not entitled; abusing a postdated check or attempts to obtain one; threatening to take judicial action without intent, right and/or ability; using false, deceptive or misleading presentation or means to collect or attempt to collect the debt; collected or attempted to collect the debt at a time or in a manner violate of the Acts; involved a person in violation of the Acts; failed to properly identify themselves; used or threatened to use violence, criminal action and obscene or offensive language, publish plaintiff's name identifying plaintiff as a person who doesn't pay debts, advertised to sell the debt to coerce payment, and/or annoyed by telephone; failed to properly identify themselves; failed to properly identify the character, amount or legal status of the debt and/or how much the collector can make through its collection; impersonated an attorney; threatened to take legal action which was illegal or to take legal action without the intent to do so; misrepresented the repercussions of the sale of a debt; informed the consumer that he committed a crime; created, disseminated and/or published any other credit information which was wrong or which defendants should have known was wrong; failed to inform that a disputed debt was disputed; used or attempted to use official looking paperwork not supported by any authority; failed to say that they were collecting a debt and that any information obtained would be used for that purpose; used or attempted to use legal process which was illegal; and in so operating its business so as to cause plaintiff damages.

11. Defendants knew, or should have known, that the information rendered, created, obtained, published, and/or disseminated was false, inaccurate and/or inappropriate and potentially damaging to plaintiff.

12. Notwithstanding this knowing falsity, defendants nonetheless rendered, disseminated, provided, made available or in some other way published such false information to third parties to plaintiff's detriment and damage.

13. As a result of the acts of defendants, plaintiff was caused to incur general and special damages.

14. Defendants' acts were so reckless, wanton, quasi-criminal and performed with such disregard for the rights of plaintiff that plaintiff demands PUNITIVE DAMAGES.

AS AND FOR A FIRST CLAIM FOR RELIEF UNDER THE ACT

15. Plaintiff repeats and realleges all previous paragraphs with the same force and effect as if the same were set forth more fully at length herein.

16. Defendants violated the Act as complained of herein and in other ways as discovery will show.

17. Such violation(s) caused plaintiff damages.

AS AND FOR A SECOND CLAIM FOR RELIEF IN LIBEL

18. Plaintiff repeats and realleges all previous paragraphs with the same force and effect as if the same were set forth more fully at length herein.

19. As a result of defendants' actions, plaintiff has been libeled and sustained damages thereby.

AS AND FOR A THIRD CLAIM FOR RELIEF IN LIBEL PER SE

20. Plaintiff repeats and realleges all previous paragraphs with the same force and effect as if the same were set forth more fully at length herein.

21. As a result of defendants' acts, plaintiff has been libeled per se and sustained per se and punitive damages.

AS AND FOR A FOURTH CLAIM FOR RELIEF IN SLANDER

22. Plaintiff repeats and realleges all previous paragraphs with the same force and effect as if the same were set forth more fully at length herein.

23. As a result of defendants' acts, plaintiff has been slandered and sustained damages thereby.

AS AND FOR A FIFTH CLAIM FOR RELIEF IN SLANDER PER SE

24. Plaintiff repeats and realleges all previous paragraphs with the same force and effect as if the same were set forth more fully at length herein.

25. As a result of defendants' acts, plaintiff has been slandered and sustained per se and punitive damages.

AS AND FOR A SEVENTH CLAIM FOR RELIEF IN FRAUD

26. Plaintiff repeats and realleges all previous paragraphs with the same force and effect as if the same were set forth more fully at length herein.

27. Defendants represented to plaintiff that they would accurately compile, maintain and/or disseminate information.

28. Such representations were false.

29. Defendants made such representations recklessly and without regard to their truth; knew them to be false; and/or had no knowledge of the truth.

30. Plaintiff relied upon these representations.

31. Plaintiff acted with ordinary prudence in relying upon such representations.

32. Such false representations injured plaintiff.

AS AND FOR AN EIGHTH CLAIM FOR RELIEF IN INJURIOUS FALSEHOOD

33. Plaintiff repeats and realleges all previous paragraphs with the same force and effect as if the same were set forth more fully at length herein.

34. As a result of defendants' acts, plaintiff has been damaged as a result of defendants communicating injurious falsehoods.

AS AND FOR A NINTH CLAIM FOR RELIEF IN INTENTIONAL INFLICTION OF EMOTIONAL DISTRESS

35. Plaintiff repeats and realleges all previous paragraphs with the same force and effect as if the same were set forth more fully at length herein.

36. As a result of defendants' intentional acts, plaintiff has suffered and continues to suffer emotional distress and other diminishments of plaintiff's quality of life.

AS AND FOR A TENTH CLAIM FOR RELIEF IN NEGLIGENT INFLICTION OF EMOTIONAL DISTRESS

37. Plaintiff repeats and realleges all previous paragraphs with the same force and effect as if the same were set forth more fully at length herein.

38. As a result of defendants' negligent acts, plaintiff has suffered and continues to suffer emotional distress and other diminishments of plaintiff's quality of life.

WHEREFORE, plaintiff demands judgment against defendants in a sum in excess of $50,000 (FIFTY THOUSAND DOLLARS) in the first claim for relief, in a sum in excess of $50,000 (FIFTY THOUSAND DOLLARS) in the second claim for relief, in a sum in excess of $50,000 (FIFTY THOUSAND DOLLARS) in the third claim for relief, in a sum in excess of $50,000 (FIFTY THOUSAND DOLLARS) in the fourth claim for relief, in a sum in excess of $50,000 (FIFTY THOUSAND DOLLARS) in the fifth claim for relief, in a sum in excess of $50,000 (FIFTY THOUSAND DOLLARS) in the sixth claim for relief, in a sum in excess of $50,00 (FIFTY THOUSAND DOLLARS) in the seventh claim for relief, in a sum in excess of $50,000 (FIFTY THOUSAND DOLLARS) in the eighth claim for relief, in the sum in excess of $50,000 (FIFTY THOUSAND DOLLARS) in the ninth claim for relief, in the sum in excess of $50,000 (FIFTY THOUSAND DOLLARS) in the tenth claim for relief, PUNITIVE DAMAGES FOR ALL CLAIMS AS SET BY THE JURY OR THE COURT, together with attorney's fees, the costs and disbursements of this action and such other relief this court may deem just and proper.

_____   _____
Signed   _Dated_

Complaint 3.
The Truth in Lending Act and the Fair Credit Reporting Act

This summons and complaint makes allegations about wrongdoing concerning both the Truth in Lending Act and the Fair Credit Reporting Act. Here again, it allows you to bring suit against more than one person. You could, for example, use this complaint against a creditor whose installment loan agreement didn't fully disclose important terms of your loan agreement and also the credit bureau that reported derogatory credit about the loan.

- In sections 9 and 10, fill in the approximate date when the lending violation occurred. If the problem is ongoing, then use the approximate date when you know it had begun, or the last time the problem happened (for example, the same error appeared on yet another copy of bill sent to you).
- In section 11, fill in the name of the person(s) who saw your report where indicated. The date refers to the date of your cover letter to the creditor/potential creditor/credit reporter in which you stated in plain English what you think it has done wrong, thereby incorporating this letter in your complaint by reference.

UNITED STATES DISTRICT COURT

_____ DISTRICT OF _____ FEDERAL COURT

_____

Plaintiff

—against—

_____

Defendant

COMPLAINT
PLAINTIFF DEMANDS
TRIAL BY JURY

Plaintiff, appearing PRO SE, hereby complains of the defendant(s) and alleges upon information and belief as follows:

Jurisdiction

1. These claims arise under Federal Question Jurisdiction, including but not limited to USC Title XV—Consumer Credit Protection Act, Subchapter, Sections 1601 et. seq.—The Truth in Lending Act (FDCPA or "Act 1"), and Sections 1681 et. seq.—The Fair Credit Reporting Act (FCRA or "Act 2") USC Title XV Sections and the law of this State where I live and where defendant(s) does(do) business, these acts hereinafter referred to collectively as Acts.

Parties

2. Plaintiff resides at _____

3. Defendant(s) is(are) a domestic corporation having its principal place of business at

Name	Address
Name	Address

ALLEGATIONS

4. Plaintiff is a consumer within the meaning and purview of the Act.

5. Defendant(s) is(are) a debt collection agency within the meaning and purview of the Act.

6. Prior to date of defendants' actions from which these allegations arise, plaintiff
    had a good credit record
    had good standing in the community
    had a job
    had a home
    had a contract to purchase a home/wanted to purchase a home
    etc.

7. Defendants, alone or in concert, joint venture, partnership and/or some other contractual arrangement, violated the Act as pled herein and as to be discovered, thus causing plaintiff special, general and punitive damages.

8. Defendants, alone or in concert, joint venture, partnership and/or some other contractual arrangement, were negligent, thus causing plaintiff damages.

9. Defendants, alone or in concert, joint venture, partnership and/or some other contractual arrangement, then illegally produced and disseminated incorrect information on or about _____, thus causing special, general and punitive damages.

10. Defendants, alone or in concert, joint venture, partnership and/or other contractual or non-contractual arrangement, produced or created, or caused to be produced or created, disseminated or published, or caused to be disseminated or published, incorrect and false information pertaining to plaintiff on or about _____ to persons identified more fully herein, causing plaintiff damages.

11. Defendants, alone or in concert, joint venture, partnership and/or some other contractual or non-contractual arrangement rendered, obtained, and/or published such information, and/or performed its obligations in a willfully and criminally reckless, negligent and/or illegal fashion in violation of the Act and the laws of this State and of these United States, in inter alia, failing to use and/or maintain reasonable procedures designed to avoid violations of Section 605 of the Fair Credit Reporting Act and/or other laws; failing to evaluate and/or re-evaluate any and all information; failing to authenticate information; disseminating such information; intentionally deceiving plaintiff who justifiably relied upon defendants' promises to plaintiff's detriment and damage, acting with malice, acting with presumed malice; acting with intent; acting with implied intent; asserting, maintaining, publishing and otherwise communicating certain false information about plaintiff; willfully failing to verify the information before publishing it; warranting, guaranteeing, representing, publishing and otherwise communicating that certain false information about plaintiff was true; breaching their contract with plaintiff, making untrue written and/or oral statements defaming, maligning and/or in other ways misrepresenting plaintiff and/or plaintiff's financial ability, status, competence, creditworthiness and/or life, publishing and/or otherwise communicating such incorrect and defamatory writing to third parties, including but not limited to _____; violating the law as detailed on the letter dated _____, sent by plaintiff to defendant, annexed hereto and incorporated by reference; and others as discovery will show; failing to check the veracity and accuracy of the information published, wantonly, willfully, recklessly and intentionally failing to use reasonable care in the course of its business; violating, inter alia, the Fair Credit Reporting Act, Title 6, Section 607(b); failing to follow reasonable procedures to assure maximum possible accuracy of

the information on plaintiff, and in so operating its business so as to cause the damages to plaintiff.

AND

Defendants, alone or in concert, joint venture, partnership and/or some other contractual or non-contractual arrangement, violated Act 1 and common law, and were negligent, reckless, wanton, quasi-criminal and deceptive in the following respects: supplying false and incorrect information, improperly computing or charging finance or any other charges, fees, premium, securities and/or escrow monies; improperly computing or charging annual or projected percentage rates; failing to inform about or accept a rescission; failing to properly transmit accurate and correct periodic statements; failing to properly identify all conditions and terms; in failing to make timely submissions; inaccurately advertising terms and conditions; and in so operating its business so as to cause injuries and damages to plaintiff.

12. Defendants knew, or should have known, that the information rendered and/or obtained, published or disseminated was false, inaccurate and/or in some way inappropriate and potentially damaging to plaintiff.

13. Notwithstanding this knowing falsity, defendants nonetheless continued to render, disseminated, provided, made available or in some other way published such false information to third parties to plaintiff's detriment and damage.

14. Defendants knew or should have known that their acts and/or omissions were or could have been damaging to plaintiff.

15. As a result of the acts of defendants, plaintiff was caused to incur general and special damages.

16. Defendants' acts were so reckless, wanton, quasi-criminal and performed with such disregard for the rights of plaintiff that plaintiff demands PUNITIVE DAMAGES.

17. Plaintiff claims no notice is necessary in all Claims for Relief alleging intentional acts. Actual and constructive is claimed with regard to all other Claims for Relief.

AS AND FOR A FIRST CLAIM FOR RELIEF UNDER THE ACT

18. Plaintiff repeats and realleges all previous paragraphs with the same force and effect as if the same were set forth more fully at length herein.

19. Defendants violated the Act as complained of herein and in other ways as discovery will show.

20. Such violation(s) caused plaintiff damages.

AS AND FOR A SECOND CLAIM FOR IN LIBEL

21. Plaintiff repeats and realleges all previous paragraphs with the same force and effect as if the same were set forth more fully at length herein.

22. As a result of defendants' actions, plaintiff has been libeled and sustained damages thereby.

AS AND FOR A THIRD CLAIM FOR RELIEF IN LIBEL PER SE

23. Plaintiff repeats and realleges all previous paragraphs with the same force and effect as if the same were set forth more fully at length herein.

24. As a result of defendants' acts, plaintiff has been libeled per se and sustained per se and punitive damages.

AS AND FOR A FOURTH CLAIM FOR RELIEF IN SLANDER

25. Plaintiff repeats and realleges all previous paragraphs with the same force and effect as if the same were set forth more fully at length herein.

26. As a result of defendants' acts, plaintiff has been slandered and sustained damages thereby.

AS AND FOR A FIFTH CLAIM FOR RELIEF IN SLANDER PER SE

27. Plaintiff repeats and realleges all previous paragraphs with the same force and effect as if the same were set forth more fully at length herein.

28. As a result of defendants' acts, plaintiff has been slandered and sustained per se and punitive damages.

AS AND FOR A SIXTH CLAIM FOR RELIEF IN DEFAMATION

29. Plaintiff repeats and realleges all previous paragraphs with the same force and effect as if the same were set forth more fully at length herein.

30. As a result of defendants' actions, plaintiff has been defamed and sustained damages thereby.

AS AND FOR A SEVENTH CLAIM FOR RELIEF IN FRAUD

31. Plaintiff repeats and realleges all previous paragraphs with the same force and effect as if the same were set forth more fully at length herein.

32. Defendants represented to plaintiff that they would accurately compile, maintain and/or disseminate information.

33. Such representations were false.

34. Defendants made such representations recklessly and without regard to their truth; knew them to be false; and/or had no knowledge of the truth.

35. Plaintiff relied upon these representations.

36. Plaintiff acted with ordinary prudence in relying upon such representations.

37. Such false representations injured plaintiff.

AS AND FOR AN EIGHTH CLAIM FOR RELIEF IN INJURIOUS FALSEHOOD

38. Plaintiff repeats and realleges all previous paragraphs with the same force and effect as if the same were set forth more fully at length herein.

39. As a result of defendants' acts, plaintiff has been damaged as a result of defendants communicating injurious falsehoods.

AS AND FOR A NINTH CLAIM FOR RELIEF IN INTENTIONAL INFLICTION OF EMOTIONAL DISTRESS

40. Plaintiff repeats and realleges all previous paragraphs with the same force and effect as if the same were set forth more fully at length herein.

41. As a result of defendants' intentional acts, plaintiff has suffered and continues to suffer emotional distress and other diminishments of plaintiff's quality of life.

AS AND FOR A TENTH CLAIM FOR RELIEF IN NEGLIGENT INFLICTION OF EMOTIONAL DISTRESS

42. Plaintiff repeats and realleges all previous paragraphs with the same force and effect as if the same were set forth more fully at length herein.

43. As a result of defendants' negligent acts, plaintiff has suffered and continues to suffer emotional distress and other diminishments of plaintiff's quality of life.

AS AND FOR AN ELEVENTH CLAIM FOR RELIEF FOR BREACH OF CONTRACT

44. Plaintiff repeats and realleges all previous paragraphs with the same force and effect as if the same were set forth more fully at length herein.

45. As a result of defendants' acts amounting to breach of contract, plaintiff has been damaged.

WHEREFORE, plaintiff demands judgment against defendants in a sum in excess of $50,000 (FIFTY THOUSAND DOLLARS) in the first claim for relief, in a sum in excess of $50,000 (FIFTY THOUSAND DOLLARS) in the second claim for relief, in a sum in excess of $50,000 (FIFTY THOUSAND DOLLARS) in the third claim for relief, in a sum in excess of $50,000 (FIFTY THOUSAND DOLLARS) in the fourth claim for relief, in a sum in excess of $50,000 (FIFTY THOUSAND DOLLARS) in the fifth claim for relief, in a sum in excess of $50,000 (FIFTY THOUSAND DOLLARS) in the sixth claim for relief, in a sum in excess of $50,000 (FIFTY THOUSAND DOLLARS) in the seventh claim for relief, in a sum in excess of $50,000 (FIFTY THOUSAND DOLLARS) in the eighth claim for relief, in the sum in excess of $50,000 (FIFTY THOUSAND DOLLARS) in the ninth claim for relief, in the sum in excess of $50,000 (FIFTY THOUSAND DOLLARS) in the tenth claim for relief, in the sum in excess of $50,000 (FIFTY THOUSAND DOLLARS) in the eleventh claim for relief; PUNITIVE DAMAGES FOR ALL CLAIMS AS SET BY THE JURY OR THE COURT, together with attorney's fees, the costs and disbursements of this action and such other relief this court may deem just and proper.

_____   _____
Signed   *Dated*

Complaint 4.
The Fair Credit Billing Act and the Fair Credit Reporting Act

This summons and complaint makes allegation about wrongdoing concerning both the Fair Credit Billing Act and the Fair Credit Reporting Act. Here again, it allows you to bring suit against more than one person. You could, for example, use this complaint against a creditor such as a credit card issuer whose billing contained errors or was sent to the wrong address, causing you to incur late marks on your credit report, and also the credit bureau that reported derogatory credit about your account.

- In sections 9 and 10, fill in the approximate date when the billing problem occurred. If the problem is ongoing, then use the approximate date when you know it had begun, or the last time the problem happened (for example, the same error appeared on yet another copy of a bill sent to you).
- In section 11, fill in: the name of the person(s) who saw your report where indicated. The date refers to the date of your cover letter to the creditor/potential creditor/credit reporter in which you stated in plain English what you think it has done wrong, thereby incorporating this letter in your complaint by reference.

UNITED STATES DISTRICT COURT

_____ DISTRICT OF _____ FEDERAL COURT

_____
Plaintiff

—against—

_____
Defendant

COMPLAINT
PLAINTIFF DEMANDS
TRIAL BY JURY

Plaintiff, appearing PRO SE, hereby complains of the defendant(s) and alleges upon information and belief as follows:

Jurisdiction

1. These claims arise under Federal Question Jurisdiction, including but not limited to USC Title XV—Consumer Credit Protection Act, Subchapter, Sections 301–306 and sec. 161 et. seq.—The Fair Credit Billing Act (FCBA or "Act 1"), and Sections 1681 et. seq.—The Fair Credit Reporting Act (FCRA or "Act 2") USC Title XV Sections and the law of this State where I live and where defendant(s) does(do) business, these acts hereinafter referred to collectively as Acts.

Parties

2. Plaintiff resides at

3. Defendant(s) is(are) a domestic corporation having its principal place of business at

_____
Name   *Address*
_____
Name   *Address*

ALLEGATIONS

4. Plaintiff is a consumer within the meaning and purview of the Act.

5. Defendant(s) is(are) a debt collection agency within the meaning and purview of the Act.

6. Prior to date of defendants' actions from which these allegations arise, plaintiff
    had a good credit record
    had good standing in the community
    had a job
    etc.

7. Defendants, alone or in concert, joint venture, partnership and/or some other contractual arrangement, violated the Act as pled herein and as to be discovered, thus causing plaintiff special, general and punitive damages.

8. Defendants, alone or in concert, joint venture, partnership and/or some other contractual arrangement, were negligent, thus causing plaintiff damages.

9. Defendants, alone or in concert, joint venture, partnership and/or some other contractual arrangement, then illegally produced and disseminated incorrect information on or about _____, thus causing special, general and punitive damages.

10. Defendants, alone or in concert, joint venture, partnership and/or other contractual or non-contractual arrangement, produced or created, or caused to be produced or created, disseminated or published, or caused to be disseminated or published, incorrect and false information pertaining to plaintiff on or about _____ to persons identified more fully herein, causing plaintiff damages.

11. Defendants, alone or in concert, joint venture, partnership and/or some other contractual or non-contractual arrangement rendered, obtained, and/or published such information, and/or performed its obligations in a willfully and criminally reckless, negligent and/or illegal fashion in violation of the Act and the laws of this State and of these United States, in inter alia, failing to use and/or maintain reasonable procedures designed to avoid violations of Section 605 of the Fair Credit Reporting Act and/or other laws; failing to evaluate and/or re-evaluate any and all information; failing to authenticate information; disseminating such information; intentionally deceiving plaintiff who justifiably relied upon defendants' promises to plaintiff's detriment and damage, acting with malice, acting with presumed malice; acting with intent; acting with implied intent; asserting, maintaining, publishing and otherwise communicating certain false information about plaintiff; willfully failing to verify the information before publishing it; warranting, guaranteeing, representing, publishing and otherwise communicating that certain false information about plaintiff was true; breaching their contract with plaintiff, making untrue written and/or oral statements defaming, maligning and/or in other ways misrepresenting plaintiff and/or plaintiff's financial ability, status, competence, creditworthiness and/or life, publishing and/or otherwise communicating such incorrect and defamatory writing to third parties, including but not limited to _____; violating the law as detailed on the letter dated _____, sent by plaintiff to defendant, annexed hereto and incorporated by reference; and others as discovery will show; failing to check the veracity and accuracy of the information published, wantonly, willfully, recklessly and intentionally failing to use reasonable care in the course of its business; violating, inter alia, the Fair Credit Reporting Act, Title 6, Section

607(b); failing to follow reasonable procedures to assure maximum possible accuracy of the information on plaintiff, and in so operating its business so as to cause the damages to plaintiff.

AND

Defendants, alone or in concert, joint venture, partnership and/or some other contractual or non-contractual arrangement, violated Act 1 and common law, and were negligent, reckless, wanton, quasi-criminal and deceptive in the following respects: in rendering, creating, supplying, disseminating, obtaining and/or publishing false information, creating, or causing to be created, publishing, disseminating or failing to discover, repair or correct billing errors, improperly reporting or threatening to report adversely on plaintiff's credit rating or standing; improperly responding to a proper directive by plaintiff; improperly restricting or closing plaintiff's account; failing to accurately assess, figure, impose, collect or attempt to collect charges, fees, premiums or other monies, failing to accurately disclose all terms and conditions; failing to promptly and correctly credit payments and/or returns; improperly using discounts; requiring the use or purchase of other services from the credit supplier as a condition; improperly offsetting or attempting to offset indebtedness; and in so operating its business so as to cause damages to plaintiff.

12. Defendants knew, or should have known, that the information rendered and/or obtained, published or disseminated was false, inaccurate and/or in some way inappropriate and potentially damaging to plaintiff.

13. Notwithstanding this knowing falsity, defendants nonetheless continued to render, disseminated, provided, made available or in some other way published such false information to third parties to plaintiff's detriment and damage.

14. Defendants knew or should have known that their acts and/or omissions were or could have been damaging to plaintiff.

15. As a result of the acts of defendants, plaintiff was caused to incur general and special damages.

16. Defendants' acts were so reckless, wanton, quasi-criminal and performed with such disregard for the rights of plaintiff that plaintiff demands PUNITIVE DAMAGES.

17. Plaintiff claims no notice is necessary in all Claims for Relief alleging intentional acts. Actual and constructive is claimed with regard to all other Claims for Relief.

AS AND FOR A FIRST CLAIM FOR RELIEF UNDER THE ACT

18. Plaintiff repeats and realleges all previous paragraphs with the same force and effect as if the same were set forth more fully at length herein.

19. Defendants violated the Act as complained of herein and in other ways as discovery will show.

20. Such violation(s) caused plaintiff damages.

AS AND FOR A SECOND CLAIM FOR RELIEF IN LIBEL

21. Plaintiff repeats and realleges all previous paragraphs with the same force and effect as if the same were set forth more fully at length herein.

22. As a result of defendants' actions, plaintiff has been libeled and sustained damages thereby.

AS AND FOR A THIRD CLAIM FOR RELIEF IN LIBEL PER SE

23. Plaintiff repeats and realleges all previous paragraphs with the same force and effect as if the same were set forth more fully at length herein.

24. As a result of defendants' acts, plaintiff has been libeled per se and sustained per se and punitive damages.

AS AND FOR A FOURTH CLAIM FOR RELIEF IN SLANDER

25. Plaintiff repeats and realleges all previous paragraphs with the same force and effect as if the same were set forth more fully at length herein.

26. As a result of defendants' acts, plaintiff has been slandered and sustained damages thereby.

AS AND FOR A FIFTH CLAIM FOR RELIEF IN SLANDER PER SE

27. Plaintiff repeats and realleges all previous paragraphs with the same force and effect as if the same were set forth more fully at length herein.

28. As a result of defendants' acts, plaintiff has been slandered and sustained per se and punitive damages.

AS AND FOR A SIXTH CLAIM FOR RELIEF IN DEFAMATION

29. Plaintiff repeats and realleges all previous paragraphs with the same force and effect as if the same were set forth more fully at length herein.

30. As a result of defendants' actions, plaintiff has been defamed and sustained damages thereby.

AS AND FOR A SEVENTH CLAIM FOR RELIEF IN FRAUD

31. Plaintiff repeats and realleges all previous paragraphs with the same force and effect as if the same were set forth more fully at length herein.

32. Defendants represented to plaintiff that it would accurately compile, maintain and/or disseminate information.

33. Such representations were false.

34. Defendants made such representations recklessly and without regard to their truth; knew them to be false; and/or had no knowledge of the truth.

35. Plaintiff relied upon these representations.

36. Plaintiff acted with ordinary prudence in relying upon such representations

37. Such false representations injured plaintiff.

AS AND FOR AN EIGHTH CLAIM FOR RELIEF IN INJURIOUS FALSEHOOD

38. Plaintiff repeats and realleges all previous paragraphs with the same force and effect as if the same were set forth more fully at length herein.

39. As a result of defendants' acts, plaintiff has been damaged as a result of defendants communicating injurious falsehoods.

AS AND FOR A NINTH CLAIM FOR RELIEF IN INTENTIONAL INFLICTION OF EMOTIONAL DISTRESS

40. Plaintiff repeats and realleges all previous paragraphs with the same force and effect as if the same were set forth more fully at length herein.

41. As a result of defendants' intentional acts, plaintiff has suffered and continues to suffer emotional distress and other diminishments of plaintiff's quality of life.

AS AND FOR A TENTH CLAIM FOR RELIEF IN NEGLIGENT INFLICTION OF EMOTIONAL DISTRESS

42. Plaintiff repeats and realleges all previous paragraphs with the same force and effect as if the same were set forth more fully at length herein.

43. As a result of defendants' negligent acts, plaintiff has suffered and continues to suffer emotional distress and other diminishments of plaintiff's quality of life.

AS AND FOR AN ELEVENTH CLAIM FOR RELIEF FOR BREACH OF CONTRACT

44. Plaintiff repeats and realleges all previous paragraphs with the same force and effect as if the same were set forth more fully at length herein.

45. As a result of defendants' acts amounting to breach of contract, plaintiff has been damaged.

WHEREFORE, plaintiff demands judgment against defendants in a sum in excess of $50,000 (FIFTY THOUSAND DOLLARS) in the first claim for relief, in a sum in excess of $50,000 (FIFTY THOUSAND DOLLARS) in the second claim for relief, in a sum in excess of $50,000 (FIFTY THOUSAND DOLLARS) in the third claim for relief, in a sum in excess of $50,000 (FIFTY THOUSAND DOLLARS) in the fourth claim for relief, in a sum in excess of $50,000 (FIFTY THOUSAND DOLLARS) in the fifth claim for relief, in a sum in excess of $50,000 (FIFTY THOUSAND DOLLARS) in the sixth claim for relief, in a sum in excess of $50,000 (FIFTY THOUSAND DOLLARS) in the seventh claim for relief, in a sum in excess of $50,000 (FIFTY THOU-SAND DOLLARS) in the eighth claim for relief, in a sum in excess of $50,000 (FIFTY THOUSAND DOLLARS) in the ninth claim for relief, in a sum in excess of $50,000 (FIFTY THOUSAND DOLLARS) in the tenth claim for relief, in a sum in excess of $50,000 (FIFTY THOUSAND DOLLARS) in the eleventh claim for relief; PUNITIVE DAMAGES FOR ALL CLAIMS AS SET BY THE JURY OR THE COURT, together with attorney's fees, the costs and disbursements of this action and such other relief this court may deem just and proper.

_____   _____
Signed   *Dated*

WAIVER OF SERVICE OF SUMMONS AND NOTICE OF LAWSUIT

If you initially send a copy of any of the preceding complaints in this section as a *notice of claim,* and your creditor still fails to respond to your dispute, it may become necessary actually to file the complaint and serve a copy on the creditor/credit bureau/collection agent, who will now be designated as the defendant in your lawsuit. Though we have described how properly to serve a summons and complaint, there is one manner of service available that won't cost you any money. This involves sending the complaint with a *waiver of service of summons and notice of lawsuit.* Though the defendant isn't obligated to sign a waiver, failure to do so will cause the court to impose the alternative service costs on the defendant, thereby relieving you of this cost.

The following two documents can be used when you actually file a lawsuit and want to serve the defendant with your summons and complaint. The Federal Rules of Civil Procedure call for parties in a lawsuit to attempt to keep down the costs of litigation. Most organizations that extend credit are likely to waive service if you send them these forms.

- The waiver. After you file your complaint with the the federal court in your district, you will be assigned a case number. You will then have all the information you need to fill in this form. On line 2, fill in <u>Your Name v. Their Name</u>. On the next lines, fill in the case number and the name of your federal district court (example: United States District Court for the <u>Southern</u> District of <u>New York</u>). Finally, add the date to the form, and sign it.
- The notice of lawsuit. Fill in the court in which you are filing your suit. Next, fill in your name above the word *Plaintiff,* and your opponent's name above the word *Defendant.* Fill in the case # where indicated. Next, repeat the name of the court in the body copy of the text. Finally, fill in the date you are sending the form and sign it.

Send two copies of the waiver. Enclose a stamped, self-addressed envelope so the defendant can return a signed copy to you.

Waiver of Service of Summons

I acknowledge receipt of your request that I waive service of a summons in the action of _____ v_____ , which is case number _____ in the United States District Court for the _____ District of _____. I have also received a copy of the complaint in the action, two copies of this instrument, and a means by which I can return the signed waiver to you without cost to me.

I agree to save the cost of service of a summons and an additional copy of the complaint in this lawsuit by not requiring that I (or the entity on whose behalf I am acting) be served with judicial process in the manner provided by Rule 4.

I (or the entity on whose behalf I am acting) will retain all defenses or objections to the lawsuit or to the jurisdiction or venue of the court except for objections based on a defect in the summons or in the service of the summons.

I understand that a judgment may be entered against me (or the entity on whose behalf I am acting) if an answer or motion under Rule 12 is not served upon you within 60 days after _____.

*Date:*_____   _____

Signature

_____

Print name

Duties to Avoid Unnecessary Costs of Service of Summons

Rule 4 of the Federal Rules of Civil Procedure requires certain parties to cooperate in saving unnecessary costs of service of the summons and complaint. A defendant located in the United States who, after being notified of an action and asked by a plaintiff located in the United States to waive service of a summons, fails to do so will be required to bear the cost of such service unless good cause be shown for its failure to sign and return the waiver.

It is not good cause for a failure to waive service that a party believe that the complaint is unfounded or that the action has been brought in an improper place or in a court that lacks jurisdiction over the subject matter of the action or over its person or property. A party who waives service of the summons retains all defenses and objections (except any relating to the summons or to the service of the summons), and may later object to the jurisdiction of the court or to the place where the action has been brought.

A defendant who waives service must within the time specified on the waiver form serve on the plaintiff's attorney a response to the complaint and must also file a signed copy of the response with the court. If the answer or motion is not served within this time, a default judgment may be taken against that defendant. By waiving service, a defendant is allowed more time to answer than if the summons had been actually served when the request for waiver of service was received.

UNITED STATES DISTRICT COURT
_____ DISTRICT OF _____

_____

Plaintiff

   —against—

_____

Defendant

NOTICE OF LAWSUIT AND
REQUEST FOR WAIVER OF
SERVICE OF SUMMONS

CASE # _____

A lawsuit has been commenced against you (or the entity on whose behalf you are addressed). A copy of the complaint is attached to this Notice. It has been filed in the United States District Court for the _____ District of _____ and has been assigned docket number _____.

This is not a formal summons or notification from the court, but rather a request that you sign and return the enclosed waiver of service in order to save the cost of serving you with a judicial summons and an additional copy of the complaint. The cost of service will be avoided if I receive a signed copy of the waiver within _Thirty (30)_ days after the date designated below as the date on which this Notice and Request is sent. I enclose a stamped and addressed envelope for your use. An extra copy of the waiver is also attached for your records.

If you comply with this request and return the signed waiver, it will be filed with the court and no summons will be served on you. The action will then proceed as if you had been served on the date the waiver is filed, except that you will not be obligated to answer the complaint before 60 days from the date designated below as the date on which this notice is sent.

If you do not return the waiver within the time indicated, I will take appropriate steps to effect formal service in a manner authorized by the Federal Rules of Civil Procedure and will then to the extent authorized by those rules, ask the Court to require you (or the party on whose behalf you are addressed) to pay the full costs of such service. In that connection, please read the statement concerning the duty of parties to waive the service of the summons, which is set forth at the foot of the waiver.

_____   _____

Signed   _Dated_

8.

LETTERS

This chapter contains the following letters:

- Cease collection letter
- Credit bureau update letter
- To credit bureau, to be sent with summons and complaint 1
- To debt collection agency, to be sent with summons and complaint 2
- To creditor—billing errors, to be sent with summons and complaint 4
- To creditor—cash for clear credit agreement, failure to change address, to be sent with summons and complaint 4
- To creditor—cash for clear credit agreement, to be sent with summons and complaint 4
- Credit bureau report request letter
- Inquiry dispute letter
- Unrated account agreement
- Credit bureau dispute letter

Avoid the look of being coached. Customize these letters by altering the wording and layout. Even add a sentence or two explaining facts or details particular to your case. Remember, this letter is not based on a formula. It is a factual statement of your position and intentions regarding the creditor. Clarity and style, while desirable, are less important than the act of letting the other side know that you believe it has made an error and that you are capable of pursuing it legally if it isn't agreeable.

Use the personal information forms (page 28–35) to record when you send this letter and the follow-up "this is the second time" letter. You may use any other phrase that reflects that you already have notified your creditor once.

Send this, and all letters in this book, by *certified/return receipt mail*. This will provide you with proof that your creditors have been notified.

Cease Collection Letter

The Fair Debt Collection Practices Act, included in full in the appendix of this book (pages 145–52), contains the guidelines under which a debt collector may attempt to get you to pay your debts. One provision in the act is extremely helpful to you in freezing your debts with the minimum pain. According to the law, you can inform your creditor that it may no longer contact you by mail or phone in regard to a particular debt. Once it has received a cease collection letter, it may contact you only once more, and only to inform you of its next step in collecting the debt, likely a threat of some type of court action. The act also includes provisions for creditor penalties should it violate your rights. To show that you are serious about enforcing your rights, you can send a copy of summons and complaint 2 (pages 93–98) as a *notice of claim* debt collection violations. You then have the ability to drop your suit as part of your bargaining chips toward a settlement that clears your debt and credit. You should be aware that as of the printing of this book, Congress is examining amendments to repeal the penalty awards for debt collection violations, on the grounds that they have provided a virtual unending source of cash for attorneys who specialize in such cases. Creditors that are losing money to those who sue under debt collection statutes are sensitive to this area of loss and will certainly pay close attention to settling any debt-restructuring issues with a consumer who is savvy in debt collection lawsuits.

Cease Collection Letter

Debt Collector's Name
Address

Your Name
Address
Debt Collector's Account # _____

Creditor's Account # *if Different* _____

Dear *Debt Collector's Name*:

I am writing to ask that you cease collection on the above account. I will no longer honor your attempts at collecting these debts. I understand that you may not contact me except to inform me of any legal action you can or will take in regard to this debt.

Best regards,

Your Name

Credit Bureau Update Letter

Credit Bureau's Name
Address

Your Name
Address

Dear *Credit Bureau's Name*:

I am writing to request that you update my account # _____.
This creditor no longer reports the derogatory credit that you have on record.
Please contact it and update my history accordingly.

Best regards,

Your Name

To Credit Bureau, to Be Sent with Summons and Complaint 1

Creditor's Name
Address
Phone Number

Dear Customer Service:

Enclosed is a summons and complaint concerning a case against your company for violation of the Fair Credit Reporting Act. I believe you have failed adequately to investigate the information on my report, specifically account _____.

Please unrate this account or I will be forced to take all necessary actions to clear my name, including pursuing any and all legal recourse necessary to accomplish this.

Regards,

Your Name

To Debt Collection Agency, to Be Sent with Summons and Complaint 2

Debt Collector's Name
Address
Phone Number

RE: Collection Account # _____
Creditor's Name

Dear *Collector or Agency's Name*:

Enclosed is a summons and complaint concerning a case against your company for violation of the Fair Credit Debt Collection Practices Act. I believe you have failed to cease collecting on my account even though I have requested this and now repeat my request. Additionally, your collection efforts are abusive. I will deal only with the original creditor on this issue.

Please unrate this account or I will be forced to take all necessary actions to clear my name, including pursuing all necessary legal recourse to accomplish this.

Regards,

Your Name

To Creditor—Billing Errors, to Be Sent with Summons and Complaint 4

Creditor's Name
Address
Phone Number

RE: Account # _____

Dear *Creditor's Name*:

Enclosed is a summons and complaint concerning a case against your company for violation of the Fair Credit Billing Act. I believe you have failed properly to bill me at my correct address, and for the correct amounts I owe. Since this is a revolving credit account, your reporting me as having paid late is in error.

Please delete the past late marks or unrate this account, or I will be forced to take all necessary actions to clear my name, including pursuing all necessary legal recourse to accomplish this.

Regards,

Your Name

To Creditor—Cash for Clear Credit Agreement, Failure to Change Address, to Be Sent with Summons and Complaint 4

Creditor's Name
Address
Phone Number

RE: Account #_____

Dear *Creditor's Name*:

Enclosed is a summons and complaint concerning a case against your company for violation of the Fair Credit Reporting and Fair Credit Billing Acts. I believe you have failed properly to bill me at my correct address, and for the correct amounts I owe. Since this is a revolving credit account, your reporting me as having paid late is in error.

I have also enclosed a restrictively endorsed check for the amount now owed. If you cash this check, you agree that my account has a zero balance, that it is closed, and that you will unrate it with all three major credit bureaus. Additionally you will send me notice of your agreement to these terms.

Regards,

Your Name

To Creditor—Cash for Clear Credit Agreement, to Be Sent with Summons and Complaint 4

Creditor's Name/Collection Agency's Name
Address
Phone Number

RE: Account #_____
and/or Collection Account #

Dear *Creditor's Name*:

Enclosed is a summons and complaint concerning a case against your company for violation of the Fair Credit Reporting and Fair Credit Billing Acts. I am willing to settle this matter, but only on the condition that you unrate my account with all three credit bureaus.

Upon receipt of your letter stating agreement to do so, I will send a restrictively endorsed check for the amount now owed. If you cash this check, you agree that my account has a zero balance, that it is closed, and that you will unrate it with all three major credit bureaus. Additionally you will send me notice of your compliance with these terms.

Regards,

Your Name

Credit Bureau Report Request Letter

Credit Bureau's Name
Address

Your Name
Address

Dear *Credit Bureau's Name*:

I am writing to request a copy of my credit report. Enclosed is a money order for $8.00. Also enclosed is a copy of my (driver's license, or social security card, or a bill from the phone or electric company).

Best regards,

Your Name

Inquiry Dispute Letter

Credit Bureau's Name
Address

Your Name
Address

Dear *Credit Bureau's Name*:

I am writing to dispute the following inquiries on my credit report. Unless these inquiries were generated from marketing programs or your list sales, they are the result of unauthorized file review. I gave none of these companies reason to believe that I would do business with them and, in fact, specifically told them not to look at my credit.

Regards,

Your Name

Unrated Account Agreement

Creditor's Name
Address

Your Name
Address

RE: Account # _____

Dear *Creditor's Name*:

As we agreed on the phone, enclosed is my payment for our settlement. As per the terms of our agreement, *choose between these options that you may have negotiated*:

1. You will freeze my interest payments and let me pay down 100 percent of the balance due, that is, $_____, in monthly installments of no less than $_____.

    OR

2. You will let me pay 100 percent of the balance due, currently at $_____, in monthly installments of no less than $_____.

    OR

3. You will let me pay 100 percent of the balance due, currently at $_____, in a lump sum.

Upon completion of the above payments, you will report nothing on credit, thus unrating my account.

Best regards,

Your Name

Credit Bureau Dispute Letter

The following letter is used to dispute items directly with the credit bureaus when negotiation with your creditors won't work. This is especially true when the creditor is the government or the IRS, or you're disputing public records.

Again, avoid the look of being coached. Customize this letter by altering the wording and layout. Even add a sentence or two explaining facts or details particular to your case. Remember, this letter is not based on a formula. It is a factual statement of your position and intentions regarding the creditor. Clarity and style, while desirable, are less important than the act of letting the other side know you believe it has made an error and that you are capable of pursuing it legally if it isn't agreeable.

Use the personal information forms (pages 28–35) to record when you send this letter and the follow-up "this is the second time" letter that you send in 30 days to enforce your request. You may use any other phrase that reflects that you already have notified your creditor once.

Send this, and all letters in this book, by *certified/return receipt mail*. This will provide you with proof that your creditors have been notified.

NOTE: *After each account name and number you are disputing, you must include a specific reason why you think that the credit entry is wrong. The reasons listed below are the more common ones, though you may list other issues. Do not, however, use an excuse such as, "I was late because I hurt my foot." The reasons that can cause a credit bureau to remove the bad credit must be rooted in the law, specifically, the Fair Credit Reporting Act.*

Reasons why an account can be wrong.

- *They didn't bill you correctly.*
- *They didn't send a bill.*
- *This item is older than seven years (ten years for bankruptcies).*
- *This is not your account.*
- *You are not responsible for this account.*
- *You paid this account on time.*

Credit Bureau Dispute Letter

Credit Bureau's Name

Your name, address, and social security number, and a copy of any of the following ID—driver's license, social security card, a phone or utility bill with the same name and address as your return address.

Dear *Credit Bureau's Name*:

The following items are incorrectly reported on my credit account. These accounts are not late, as reported. Please correct or delete. [*Add reason why account is wrong here.*] You are obligated to look at the underlying circumstances of this account and not merely rereport what you are told.

    ACCOUNT NAMES: ACCOUNT NUMBERS:
    1.
    2.
    etc.

Best regards,

Your Name

9.

MORE CREDIT TOPICS

 These topics don't fit in other sections of the book, but they are important. If you would like more information on these or any other credit issues, write the authors (see page 6) and we will add your name to our mailing list.

IRS SETTLEMENT NEGOTIATION

As we said earlier, the IRS is one creditor that can't be ignored. It can empty your bank account, garnishee your wages, and seize your house. Whatever can be sold is fair game. The IRS is notorious for collecting what it thinks you owe, whether you actually do or not, and it is up to you to prove otherwise. Guilty until proven innocent, you pay first and fight to regain your loss. Instead of letting the government bulldoze you, it's best to negotiate payment.

There are two IRS settlement methods covered here. The first is an *installment agreement*. This is used to prevent the IRS from attaching a lien to your property by making a workable plan on paying money you acknowledge is owed. The second is a *settlement agreement*, in which the IRS typically takes 25 to 33 percent of your total debt and wipes the slate clean. To achieve this agreement, you must demonstrate why you can't pay all you owe and why future income is unlikely to settle your tax debt.

IRS Installment Agreement

To begin the process of reaching an installment agreement, you need IRS form 433-A, an information collection statement for individuals. Businesses use form 433-B. Form 433 asks for general information about your income, assets, and credit lines.

To prepare a payment plan using 433-A, you must establish two financial components: (1) what you have in equity and (2) what you have left in income each month after expenses. To determine your equity in assets, first determine a value for each individual asset. When making the IRS an offer, equity is calculated on the *quick sale* value of each asset less encumbrances that have priority over a federal tax lien, such as a bank mortgage agreement. The quick sale value is uniquely used for settling with the IRS. This method acknowledges that the taxpayer and the IRS are in opposition and seeks to negotiate a middle ground valuation for your property.

Two common appraisal methods are *fair market value* and *forced liquidation value. Fair market value* is the price struck between a willing seller and willing buyer for an asset reasonably marketed over a sufficient period of time—it's the maximum price obtainable for the asset in a "normal" market. *Forced liquidation value* represents the amount obtained in a distress sale, for example, a public auction. The quick sale value is reached by negotiation between you and the IRS, and is generally a compromise between these two valuation methods. We suggest that you make an offer based on liquidation value and expect an IRS counteroffer that modifies it upward. The end price will likely fall between 20 and 50 percent off fair market. The exact price will depend in part on how unusual or difficult it is to sell the item in question.

Two types of assets have unique valuation problems. The first, *jointly held property,* generally requires a valuation of a quick sale discount minus approximately 30 percent. The second, a *pension plan,* may have no value if you can't draw against it until you leave your job or retire. If you can borrow from your plan, that amount will be considered equity. The value of an IRA or a Keogh is calculated after penalties for early withdrawal, sometimes as much as 50 percent less than book value.

Once asset value is determined, you still have to figure your monthly cash flow after living expenses. Form 433-A is used to compute this amount. In the first column of the form's page 4, enter all income. For wages, enter gross income before withholding, not take-home pay. In the expenses area, remember to include all taxes withheld from your paycheck (line 46).

Using a book titled *National Standard Expenses* (available at your local library), your expenses on *personal items* (clothing, housekeeping, and grooming, among others) are determined by how many people your household supports. *Housing & utilities* expenses are based on county averages, and *transportation* cost is based on no more than two cars and calculated against national averages. At the end, each of these categories is figured on either actual or standard expenses, whichever is lower.

By subtracting your allowable expenses from your income, and adding the resulting figure to your quick sale equity, you arrive at the sum to offer the IRS. Armed with this information, you can now complete form 433.

Next comes the game: The IRS will try to disallow some of your expenses in an effort to get the highest installment payment possible. Be prepared to defend all you claim as *reasonable and necessary*. If you can convince the IRS that your cash flow is zero or negative, that is, you spend as much or more than you make in order to survive, you may not have to pay anything out of your future income. After liquidating your equity at quick sale prices, the remaining debt could be considered uncollectible. Your account would be considered a hardship case or, using IRS parlance, you'd be "53'd."

No matter what you finally agree on with the IRS, *don't ever make the mistake of paying late*. Do so more than twice and you invalidate your agreement.

Settlement Agreement

The IRS is particularly interested in bringing taxpayers back into the fold. Their experience indicates that filing a lien against someone often pushes that person out of the system. By offering a fresh start through a compromise, the IRS increases its base of taxpayers, since those who take advantage of settlements do so with the condition that they comply with the law by filing and paying taxes. To woo you back onto the tax roles, the IRS will accept as little as 10 cents on the dollar. An *offer-in-compromise,* as IRS settlements are known, can be filed by any taxpaying entity no matter the type, combination, or age of the back tax.

There are two types of compromise offers. The first, *doubt to collectability,* arises when you can't predictably pay what you owe in the near future. The second, *doubt to liability,* concerns taxes you don't believe you owe. As this implies, you pay now and fight later. In figuring the compromise, just as in the installment agreement, you need to figure your asset equity and earnings above living expenses. Settlements can be made in installments, generally over a period of two years or less. Lump-sum settlements likely get you the best discount.

Settling can help you avoid bankruptcy and has the added advantage of not showing up on your credit report. Also, filing an offer-in-compromise suspends collection action while your negotiation is underway—no tax agent will storm your house and bank account. The process takes four to six months to complete.

If you fail to file and pay taxes within the next five years, the settlement can be invalidated. As with all IRS settlements, they will challenge your expenses and you'll need to defend them. If your revenue officer hints that he or she may reject your offer, don't be dismayed. This is an attempt to dissuade your seeking a settlement the IRS doesn't like, though it will likely agree at the end. Remember: Hold your ground on the validity of expenses and the amount of your settlement offer. These deals are done all the time, and your opponent is as interested in moving on as you are. Finally, when dealing with the IRS, an accountant experienced in these settlements may be of great service, especially if you haven't much experience in negotiation.

AUTO REPOSSESSION

If you are having trouble keeping current with your car loan, you may face losing your car to repossession. Depending on the state you live in, the rules governing your rights should your car be taken by a lender may vary considerably. You could, for instance, be liable for the difference between what you owe and what the car is sold for. This amount is often determined by a *deficiency judgment* that a lender gets a court to render against you. A lender can't take your car, sell it for substantially less than it is worth, and charge you the difference. Still, a car generally does lose much of its value more quickly than its quick sale price at a *commercially reasonable* rate. In some jurisdictions, you can *reinstate* your loan by paying your arrears. Other locales dictate that a lender must notify you of the auction in which you car will be sold so you can bid on it.

Since car repossession can be abused, many states have laws to protect consumers. Some states allow constant late payers to assume that this has been accepted by the lender as renegotiated payment terms. You can also negotiate for new payment terms and, so long as they are kept, avoid repossession.

YOUR HOME

Deed in-Lieu-of Foreclosure

Lenders aren't generally real estate agents, and they don't want to foreclose on your home. Still, they are governed by forces other than your ability to repay. Some mortgages are actually part of a package of mortgage-backed securities. A lender may be obligated to begin foreclosure after three missed payments. If you are facing the loss of your home, you can surrender your *deed in-lieu-of foreclosure.* This is a viable option especially on a second property. Though this is a last resort, it will stop a foreclosure from appearing on your credit report. If you won't have anywhere to live, you may want to stop and fight it out.

Mortgage Negotiation Technique

If you are already late with your mortgage, you can use the forms in this book, or a lawyer, to raise legal disputes under the Truth in Lending Act to push for repair of your credit. Possibly the terms of interest aren't clearly or accurately explained. By raising bargaining chips before you can resume payment, you can have past delinquent credit cleared or unrated as part of your settlement. Though you may not have the legal understanding to find the flaws in a mortgage contract, communicating with your lender about your belief that the contract does violate TILA will certainly catch its attention. There are lawyers who specialize in making just this sort of foray with the intent of using potential TILA violation against the lender. This sort of violation does indeed happen and is a lot more common than you may believe. In fact, many large lending organizations have, over the last decade, been called to task for overcharging consumers on fees or percentages, or for poorly disclosing the actual mortgage costs in their contracts.

MODERN COLLECTION BUSINESS

In recent years, debt collection has become a science. By calling consumers on holidays, during snowstorms, or when the Super Bowl is on, for example, the collectors are able to begin reaching even the most evasive debtors. With a record one-million-plus households filing bankruptcy last year, the bill collection business continues to grow by leaps and bounds.

Old-fashioned techniques such as tough guy threats and dunning notices seem to have lost their punch. Consequently, a new breed of collector has appeared. These "friendly financial adviser" types now ask how they can help rather than just demand the money. The traditional collection procedure of ignoring what the consumer says and continually asking for the cash, known as "grinding," doesn't seem to work with the newest and youngest breed of debtors, who are characterized as avoiding responsibility whenever possible.

Collection efforts have even been shifted to the very recent late payer. Known as an "early out" program, creditors hire collection agents to call after only one missed payment, with the idea that they can nip further delinquency in the bud.

Automated dialing and other computerized collection processes have enabled companies to contact huge numbers of delinquent debtors, with larger collection agencies dialing out over 100,000 times a day. A collector will have one person on the line while the computer dials the next with a recorded message that asks him or her to hold until the first call is done. This depersonalized process allows collection personnel to spend more of their time asking for money. With collection personnel making $9 to $11 per hour plus commission, it isn't hard to fathom why highly motivated, computer-driven collection agencies constitute the fastest-growing small business niche in the country. Further fueling this explosive growth is a record $100 billion in debt assigned to collection agencies in 1995, with roughly a third recovered.

The people best suited to collecting have assertive personalities, a dash of cynicism, and a sales background. They are empathetic but firm, attentive listeners but willing to challenge. Some collectors report that they enjoy a good head game. On the job, they learn skip-tracing skills to find evasive consumers who change addresses, phone numbers, and even names in an effort to avoid paying.

CREDIT SCORING

Credit scoring was generally limited to credit card applications until about 1996. In that year, federal lending guidelines were enacted that made mortgages with federal connections use credit scoring on new applications. Credit scoring judges the risk associated with lending based on payment history from existing credit lines. The procedure has no limits on what can and cannot be evaluated to arrive at a final credit score.

Financial scoring isn't new. In the 1960s and 1970s, statistical analysis was designed to predict the movement of stocks. Several companies claimed that computer-chosen portfolios could outperform the stock market and enrich their users. As with any attempt to predict the future, the programs failed miserably, yielding worse results than random guessing. Without learning their lesson, computer programmers have now sold their promises to federal regulators who apparently also forgot the last round. Credit reports are the source of more consumer complaints than any other category for the last five years straight. Though the *Credit Reform Act of 1994* was drafted, it never became law. The FTC was supposed to gain the ability to regulate scoring in this legislation, but failure to update existing credit laws have left the issue in limbo.

Excerpt from an FTC Press Release

. . . As it stands now victims of this scheme do not even have the right to know if they were denied credit by a machine or a human, let alone review or challenge the scores involved. Industry publications estimate over 85 percent of all consumer-credit-granting decisions are made by computer. With the new federal regulations requiring it, that number will hit 99 percent in no time. And Congress grants no protection at all to victims of credit scoring, insisting that you can "fix" credit reporting problems by attaching a cute little note to a credit file that will never be seen by human eyes. Thousands of American victims can only reply "Yeah. Right."

How can we protect ourselves? We can't. At this time U.S. citizens have no real protection, but that doesn't mean it can't be done. Most democracies, including England, France, and the Netherlands, have essentially outlawed credit reports as Americans know them since the 1970s, and have thriving economies. In fact, countries that have outlawed blacklists (i.e., credit reports) have managed to end up owning a huge share of our banks. For the time being, we are the only country without meaningful protection against credit reports and "ghost scoring" (Canada plays a close second). With no way to find out what factors are used or even *if* a scoring system is in use, we lose credit cards and homes simply because a paycheck did not arrive when a computer assumed it should or a third cousin we've never met declares bankruptcy. Even a change of buying habits (buying a cheaper roll of toilet paper could cost you your home) can destroy your credit and you will never be told why.

Credit Bureau Scores and Fair Isaac Company

In the last ten years Experian, Equifax, and Trans Union hired the Fair Isaac Company to create a scoring system that supposedly would determine delinquency risk in credit applicants. Each credit bureau uses the Fair Isaac model (known as the FICO) to produce its own rating. Since the different bureaus often have divergent credit reports, an individual's credit score is likely to differ among the three credit bureaus.

To develop a scoring model, the credit bureaus each provided Fair Isaac with a very large random sample of credit files, with each selected consumer's file compared between the present and two years ago. Those who had latenesses in the last two years were separated from those who paid on time. Using these two groups, a number of characteristics that might predict delinquent behavior were identified and thus used in credit scoring.

A credit grantor examines the likelihood of eliminating good customers, while considering the advantage of eliminating risky customers in order to establish a cut-off score. Since the factors that influence the score are always changing, it is calculated at the time a report is issued. There's no way to adjust the score by hand, so inaccurate credit information is difficult to exclude whether the lender knows of the mistake or not. And that's the problem with computer scoring in a nutshell. Its inflexibility can produce poor, overly restrictive lending decisions.

10.

THE CREDIT LAWS

FAIR CREDIT REPORTING ACT (FCRA)

The FCRA provides the basic tools for credit repair. It is badly in need of updating to regulate the credit bureaus; in the absence of reform from Congress, most progress has been made by state attorneys general in court. The repair section makes extensive use of the act, but it may help to read the actual law, included here in full for you.

"Title VI—Provisions Relating to Credit Reporting Agencies

"*Amendment of Consumer Credit Protection Act*

"Sec. 601. The Consumer Credit Protection Act is amended by adding at the end thereof the following new title:

"Title VI—Consumer Credit Reporting

"Sec. 601. Short title

"This title may be cited as the Fair Credit Reporting Act.

"Sec. 602. Findings and purpose

"(a) The Congress makes the following findings:

"(1) The banking system is dependent upon fair and accurate credit reporting. Inaccurate credit reports directly impair the efficiency of the banking system, and unfair credit reporting methods undermine the public confidence which is essential to the continued functioning of the banking system.

"(2) An elaborate mechanism has been developed for investigating and evaluating the credit worthiness, credit standing, credit capacity, character, and general reputation of consumers.

"(3) Consumer reporting agencies have assumed a vital role in assembling and evaluating consumer credit and other information on consumers.

"(4) There is a need to insure that consumer reporting agencies exercise their grave responsibilities with fairness, impartiality and a respect for the consumer's right to privacy.

"(b) It is the purpose of this title to require that consumer reporting agencies adopt reasonable procedures for meeting the needs of commerce for consumer credit, personnel, insurance, and other information in a manner which is fair and equitable to the consumer, with regard to the confidentiality, accuracy, relevancy and proper utilization of such information in accordance with the requirements of this title.

"Sec. 603. Definitions and rules of construction

"(a) Definitions and rules of construction set forth in this section are applicable for the purposes of this title.

"(b) The term 'person' means any individual, partnership, corporation, trust, estate, cooperative, association, government or governmental subdivision or agency, or other entity.

"(c) The term 'consumer' means an individual.

"(d) The term 'consumer report' means any written, oral, or other communication of any information by a consumer reporting agency bearing on a consumer's credit worthiness, credit standing, credit capacity, character, general reputation, personal characteristics, or mode of living which is used or expected to be used or collected in whole or in part for the purpose of serving as a factor in establishing the consumer's eligibility for (1) credit or insurance to be used primarily for personal, family, or household purposes, or (2) employment purposes, or (3) other purposes authorized under section 604. The term does not include (A) any report containing information solely as to transactions or experiences between the consumer and the person making the report; (B) any authorization or approval of a specific extension of credit directly or indirectly by the issuer of a credit card or similar device; or (C) any report in which a person who has been requested by a third party to make a specific extension of credit directly or indirectly to a consumer conveys his decision with respect to such

request, if the third party advises the consumer of the name and address of the person to whom the request was made and such person makes the disclosures to the consumer required under section 615.

"(e) The term 'investigative consumer report' means a consumer report or portion thereof in which information on a consumer's character, general reputation, personal characteristics, or mode of living is obtained through personal interviews with neighbors, friends, or associates of the consumer reported on or with others with whom he is acquainted or who may have knowledge concerning any such items of information. However, such information shall not include specific factual information on a consumer's credit record obtained directly from a creditor of the consumer or from a consumer reporting agency when such information was obtained directly from a creditor of the consumer or from the consumer.

"(f) The term 'consumer reporting agency' means any person which, for monetary fees, dues, or on a cooperative nonprofit basis, regularly engages in whole or in part in the practice of assembling or evaluating consumer credit information or other information on consumers for the purpose of furnishing consumer reports to third parties, and which uses any means of facility of interstate commerce for the purpose of preparing or furnishing consumer reports.

"(g) The term 'file' when used in connection with information on any consumer means all of the information on that consumer recorded and retained by a consumer reporting agency regardless of how the information is stored.

"(h) The term 'employment purposes' when used in connection with a consumer report means a report used for the purpose of evaluating a consumer for employment, promotion, reassignment, or retention as an employee.

"(i) The term 'medical information'

means information or records obtained, with the consent of the individual to whom it relates, from licensed physicians or medical practitioners, hospitals, clinics, or other medical or medically related facilities.

"Sec. 604. Permissible purposes of reports

"A consumer reporting agency may furnish a consumer report under the following circumstances and no other:

"(1) In response to the order of a court having jurisdiction to issue such an order.

"(2) In accordance with the written instructions of the consumer to whom it relates.

"(3) To a person which it has reason to believe—

"(A) intends to use the information in connection with a credit transaction involving the consumer on whom the information is to be furnished and involving the extension of credit to, or review or collection of an account of, the consumer; or

"(B) intends to use the information for employment purposes; or

"(C) intends to use the information in connection with the underwriting of insurance involving the consumer; or

"(D) intends to use the information in connection with a determination of the consumer's eligibility for a license or other benefit granted by a governmental instrumentality required by law to consider an applicant's financial responsibility or status; or

"(E) otherwise has a legitimate business need for the information in connection with a business transaction involving the consumer.

"Sec. 605. Obsolete information

"(a) Except as authorized under subsection (b), no consumer reporting agency may make any consumer report containing any of the following items of information:

"(1) Cases under title 11 of the United States Code or under the Bankruptcy Act that, from the date of entry of the order for relief or the date of adjudication, as the cause may be, antedate the report by more than 10 years.

"(2) Suits and judgments which, from date of entry, antedate the report by more than seven years or until the governing statute of limitations has expired, whichever is the longer period.

"(3) Paid tax liens which, from date of payment, antedate the report by more than seven years.

"(4) Accounts placed for collection or charged to profit and loss which antedate the report by more than seven years.

"(5) Records of arrest, indictment, or conviction of crime which, from date of disposition, release, or parole, antedate the report by more than seven years.

"(6) Any other adverse item of information which antedates the report by more than seven years.

"(b) The provisions of subsection (a) are not applicable in the case of any consumer credit report to be used in connection with—

"(1) a credit transaction involving, or which may reasonably be expected to involve, a principal amount of $50,000 or more;

"(2) the underwriting of life insurance involving, or which may reasonably be expected to involve, a face amount of $50,000 or more; or

"(3) the employment of any individual at an annual salary which equals, or which may reasonably be expected to equal $20,000, or more.

"Sec. 606. Disclosure of investigative consumer reports

"(a) A person may not procure or cause to be prepared an investigative consumer report on any consumer unless—

"(1) it is clearly and accurately disclosed to the consumer that an investigative consumer report including information as to his character, general reputation, personal characteristics, and mode of living, whichever are applicable, may be made, and such disclosure (A) is made in a writing mailed, or otherwise delivered, to the consumer, not later than three days after the date on which the report was first requested, and (B) includes a statement informing the consumer of his right to request the additional disclosures provided for under subsection (b) of this section; or

"(2) the report is to be used for employment purposes for which the consumer has not specifically applied.

"(b) Any person who procures or causes to be prepared an investigative consumer report on any consumer shall, upon written request made by the consumer within a reasonable period of time after the receipt by him of the disclosure required by subsection (a) (1), make a complete and accurate disclosure of the nature and scope of the investigation requested. This disclosure shall be made in a writing mailed, or otherwise delivered, to the consumer not later than five days after the date on which the request for such disclosure was received from the consumer or such report was first requested, whichever is the later.

"(c) No person may be held liable for any violation of subsection (a) or (b) of this section if he shows by a preponderance of the evidence that at the time of the violation he maintained reasonable procedures to assure compliance with subsection (a) or (b).

"Sec. 607. Compliance procedures

"(a) Every consumer reporting agency shall maintain reasonable procedures designed to avoid violations of section 605 and to limit the furnishing of consumer reports to the purposes listed under section 604. These procedures shall require that prospective users of the information identify themselves, certify the purposes for which the information is sought, and certify that the information will be used for no other purpose. Every consumer reporting agency shall make a reasonable effort to verify the identity of a new prospective user and the uses certified by such prospective user prior to furnishing such user a consumer report. No consumer reporting agency may furnish a consumer report to any person if it has reasonable grounds for believing that the consumer report will not be used for a purpose listed in section 604.

"(b) Whenever a consumer reporting agency prepares a consumer report it shall follow reasonable procedures to assure maximum possible accuracy of the information concerning the individual about whom the report relates.

"Sec. 608. Disclosures to governmental agencies

"Notwithstanding the provisions of section 604, a consumer reporting agency may furnish identifying information respecting any consumer, limited to his name, address, former addresses, places of employment, or former places of employment, to a governmental agency.

"Sec. 609. Disclosures to consumers

"(a) Every consumer reporting agency shall, upon request and proper identification of any consumer, clearly and accurately disclose to the consumer:

"(1) The nature and substance of all information (except medical information) in its files on the consumer at the time of the request.

"(2) The sources of the information; except that the sources of information acquired solely for use in preparing an investigative consumer report and actually used for no other purpose need not be disclosed. Provided, That in the event an action is brought under this title, such sources shall be available to the plaintiff under appropriate discovery procedures in the court in which the action is brought.

"(3) The recipients of any consumer report on the consumer which it has furnished—

"(A) for employment purposes within the two-year period preceding the request, and

"(B) for any other purpose within the six-month period preceding the request.

"(b) The requirements of subsection (a) respecting the disclosure of sources of information and the recipients of consumer reports do not apply to information received or consumer reports furnished prior to the effective date of this title except to the extent that the matter involved is contained in the files of the consumer reporting agency on that date.

"Sec. 610. Conditions of disclosure to consumers

"(a) A consumer reporting agency shall make the disclosures required under section 609 during normal business hours and on reasonable notice.

"(b) The disclosures required under section 609 shall be made to the consumer—

"(1) in person if he appears in person and furnishes proper identification; or

"(2) by telephone if he has made a written request, with proper identification, for telephone disclosure and the toll charge, if any, for the telephone call is prepaid by or charged directly to the consumer.

"(c) Any consumer reporting agency shall provide trained personnel to explain to the consumer any information furnished to him pursuant to section 609.

"(d) The consumer shall be permitted to be accompanied by one other person of his choosing, who shall furnish reasonable identification. A consumer reporting agency may require the consumer to furnish a written statement granting permission to the consumer reporting agency to discuss the consumer's file in such person's presence.

"(e) Except as provided in sections 616 and 617, no consumer may bring any action or proceeding in the nature of defamation, invasion of privacy, or negligence with respect to the reporting of information against any consumer reporting agency, any user of information, or any person who furnishes information to a consumer reporting agency, based on information disclosed pursuant to section 609, 610, or 615, except as to false information furnished with malice or willful intent to injure such consumer.

"Sec. 611. Procedure in case of disputed accuracy

"(a) If the completeness or accuracy of any item of information contained in his file is disputed by a consumer, and such dispute is directly conveyed to the consumer reporting agency by the consumer, the consumer reporting agency shall within a reasonable period of time reinvestigate and record the current status of that information unless it has reasonable grounds to believe that the dispute by the consumer is frivolous or irrelevant. If after such reinvestigation such information is found to be inaccurate or can no longer be verified, the consumer reporting agency shall promptly delete such information. The presence of contradictory information in the consumer's file does not in and of itself constitute reasonable grounds for believing the dispute is frivolous or irrelevant.

"(b) If the reinvestigation does not resolve the dispute, the consumer may file a brief statement setting forth the nature of the dispute. The consumer reporting agency may limit such statements to not more than one hundred words if it provides the consumer with assistance in writing a clear summary of the dispute.

"(c) Whenever a statement of a dispute is filed, unless there is reasonable grounds to believe that it is frivolous or irrelevant, the consumer reporting agency shall, in any subsequent consumer report containing the information in question, clearly note that it is disputed by the consumer and provide either the consumer's statement or a clear and accurate codification or summary thereof.

"(d) Following any deletion of information which is found to be inaccurate or whose accuracy can no longer be verified or any notation as to disputed information, the consumer reporting agency shall, at the request of the consumer, furnish notification that the item has been deleted or the statement, codification, or summary pursuant to subsection (b) or (c) to any person specifically designated by the consumer who has within two years prior thereto received a consumer report for employment purposes, or within six months prior thereto received a consumer report for any other purpose, which contained the deleted or disputed information. The consumer reporting agency shall clearly and conspicuously disclose to the consumer his rights to make such a request. Such disclosure shall be made at or prior to the time the information is deleted or the consumer's statement regarding the disputed information is received.

"Sec. 612. Charges for certain disclosures

"A consumer reporting agency shall make all disclosures pursuant to section 609 and furnish all consumer reports pursuant to section 611 (d) without charge to the consumer if, within thirty days after receipt by such consumer of a notification pursuant to section 615 or notification from a debt collection agency affiliated with such consumer reporting agency stating that the consumer's credit rating may be or has been adversely affected, the consumer makes a request under section 609 or 611 (d). Otherwise, the consumer reporting agency may impose a reasonable charge on the consumer for making disclosure to such consumer pursuant to section 609, the charge for which shall be indicated to the consumer prior to making disclosure; and for furnishing notifications, statements, summaries, or codifications to person designated by the consumer pursuant to section 611 (d), the charge for which shall be indicated to the consumer prior to furnishing such information, and shall not exceed the charge that the consumer reporting agency would impose on each designated recipient for a consumer report except that no charge may be made for notifying such persons of the deletion of information which is found to be inaccurate or which can no longer be verified.

"Sec. 613. Public record information for employment purposes

"A consumer reporting agency which furnishes a consumer report for employment purposes and which for that purpose compiles and reports items of information on consumers which are matters of public record and are likely to have an adverse effect upon a consumer's ability to obtain employment shall—

"(1) at the time such public record information is reported to the user of such consumer report, notify the consumer of the fact that public record information is being reported by the consumer reporting agency, together with the name and address of the person to whom such information is being reported; or

"(2) maintain strict procedures designed to insure that whenever public record information which is likely to have an adverse effect on a consumer's ability to obtain employment is reported it is complete and up to date. For purposes of this paragraph, items of public record relating to arrest, indictments, convictions, suits, tax liens, and outstanding judgments shall be considered up to date if the current public record status of the item at the time of the report is reported.

"Sec. 614. Restrictions on investigative consumer reports

"Whenever a consumer reporting agency prepares an investigative consumer report, no adverse information in the consumer report (other than information which is a matter of public record) may be included in a subsequent consumer report unless such adverse information has been verified in the process of making such subsequent consumer report, or the adverse information was received within the three-month period preceding the date the subsequent report is furnished.

"Sec. 615. Requirements on users of consumer reports

"(a) Whenever credit or insurance for personal, family, or household purposes, or employment involving a consumer is denied or the charge for such credit or insurance is increased either wholly or partly because of information contained in a consumer report from a consumer reporting agency, the user of the consumer report shall so advise the consumer against whom such adverse action has been taken and supply the name and address of the consumer reporting agency making the report.

"(b) Whenever credit for personal, family, or household purposes involving a consumer is denied or the charge for such credit is increased either wholly or partly because of information obtained from a person other than a consumer reporting agency bearing upon the consumer's credit worthiness, credit standing, credit capacity, character, general reputation, personal characteristics, or mode of living, the user of such information shall, within a reasonable period of time, upon the consumer's written request for the reasons for such adverse action received within sixty days after learning of such adverse action, disclose the nature of the information to the consumer. The user of such information shall clearly and accurately disclose to the consumer his right to make such written requests at the time such adverse action is communicated to the consumer.

"(c) No person shall be held liable for any violation of this section if he shows by a preponderance of the evidence that at the time of the alleged violation he maintained reasonable procedures to assure compliance with the provisions of subsections (a) and (b).

"Sec. 616. Civil liability for willful noncompliance

"Any consumer reporting agency or user of information which willfully fails to comply with any requirement imposed under this title with respect to any consumer is liable to that consumer in an amount equal to the sum of—

"(1) any actual damages sustained by the consumer as a result of the failure;

"(2) such amount of punitive damages as the court may allow; and

"(3) in the case of any successful action to enforce any liability under this section, the costs of the action together with reasonable attorney's fees as determined by the court.

"Sec. 617. Civil liability for negligent noncompliance

"Any consumer reporting agency or user of information which is negligent in failing to comply with any requirement imposed under this title with respect to any consumer is liable to that consumer in an amount equal to the sum of—

"(1) any actual damages sustained by the consumer as a result of the failure;

"(2) in the case of any successful action to enforce any liability under this section, the costs of the action together with reasonable attorney's fees as determined by the court.

"Sec. 618. Jurisdiction of courts; limitation of actions

"An action to enforce any liability created under this title may be brought in any appropriate United States district court without regard to the amount in controversy, or in any other court of competent jurisdiction, within two years from the date on which the liability arises, except that where a defendant has materially and willfully misrepresented any information required under this title to be disclosed to an individual and the information so misrepresented is material to the establishment of the defendant's liability to that individual under this title, the action may be brought at any time within two years after discovery by the individual of the misrepresentation.

"Sec. 619. Obtaining information under false pretenses

"Any person who knowingly and willfully obtains information on a consumer from a consumer reporting agency under false pretense shall be fined not more than $5,000 or imprisoned not more than one year, or both.

"Sec. 620. Unauthorized disclosures by officers or employees

"Any officer or employee of a consumer reporting agency who knowingly and willfully provides information concerning an individual from the agency's files to a person not authorized to receive that information

shall be fined not more than $5,000 or imprisoned not more than one year, or both.

"Sec. 621. Administrative enforcement

"(a) Compliance with the requirements imposed under this title shall be enforced under the Federal Trade Commission Act by the Federal Trade Commission with respect to consumer reporting agencies and all other persons subject thereto, except to the extent that enforcement of the requirements imposed under this title is specifically committed to some other government agency under subsection (b) hereof. For the purpose of the exercise by the Federal Trade Commission Act, a violation of any requirement or prohibition imposed under this title shall constitute an unfair or deceptive act or practice in commerce in violation of section 5 (a) of the Federal Trade Commission pursuant to this subsection, irrespective of whether that person is engaged in commerce or meets any other jurisdictional tests in the Federal Trade Commission Act. The Federal Trade Commission shall have such procedural, investigative, and enforcement powers, including the power to issue procedural rules in enforcing compliance with the requirements imposed under this title and to require the filing of reports, the production of documents, and the appearance of witnesses as though the applicable terms and conditions of the Federal Trade Commission Act were part of this title. Any person violating any of the provisions of this title shall be subject to the penalties and entitled to the privileges and immunities provided in the Federal Trade Commission Act as though the applicable terms and provisions thereof were part of this title.

"(b) Compliance with the requirements imposed under this title with respect to consumer reporting agencies and persons who use consumer reports from such agencies shall be enforced under—

"(1) section 8 of the Federal Deposit Insurance Act, in the case of:

"(A) national banks, by the Comptroller of the Currency;

"(B) member banks of the Federal Reserve Board; and

"(C) banks insured by the Federal Deposit Insurance Corporation (other than members of the Federal Reserve System), by the Board of Directors of the Federal Deposit Insurance Corporation.

"(2) section 5 (d) of the Home Owners Loan Act of 1933, section 407 of the National Housing Act, and sections 6 (i) and 17 of the Federal Home Loan Bank Act, by the Federal Home Loan Bank Board (acting directly or through the Federal Savings and Loan Insurance Corporation), in the case of any institution subject to any of those provisions;

"(3) the Federal Credit Union Act, by the Administrator of the National Credit Union Administration with respect to any Federal credit union;

"(4) the Acts to regulate commerce, by the Interstate Commerce Commission with respect to any common carrier subject to those Acts;

"(5) the Federal Aviation Act of 1958, by the Civil Aeronautics Board with respect to any air carrier or foreign air carrier subject to that Act; and

"(6) the Packers and Stockyards Act, 1921 (except as provided in section 406 of that Act), by the Secretary of Agriculture with respect to any activities subject to that Act.

"(c) For the purpose of the exercise by any agency referred to in subsection (b) of its powers under any Act referred to in that subsection, a violation of any requirement imposed under this title shall be deemed to be a violation of a requirement imposed under that Act. In addition to its powers under any provision of law specifically referred to in that subsection may exercise, for the purpose of enforcing compliance with any requirement imposed under this title any other authority conferred on it by law.

"Sec. 622. Relation to State laws

"This title does not annul, alter, affect, or exempt any person subject to the provisions of this title from complying with the laws of any State with respect to the collection, distribution, or use of any information on consumers, except to the extent that those laws are inconsistent with any provision of this title, and then only to the extent of the inconsistency."

FAIR DEBT COLLECTION PRACTICES (FDCP)

You'll appreciate the FDCP if there's a collection agency harassing you. It is quite specific about what kind of collection tactics are illegal.

"Subchapter V—Debt Collection Practices

" § 1692. Congressional findings and declaration of purpose

"(a) There is abundant evidence of the use of abusive, deceptive, and unfair debt collection practices by many debt collectors. Abusive debt collection practices contribute to the number of personal bankruptcies, to marital instability, to the loss of jobs, and to invasions of individual privacy.

"(b) Existing laws and procedures for redressing these injuries are inadequate to protect consumers.

"(c) Means other than misrepresentation or other abusive debt collection practices are available for the effective collection of debts.

"(d) Abusive debt collection practices are carried on to a substantial extent in interstate commerce and through means and instrumentalities of such commerce. Even where abusive debt collection practices are purely intrastate in character, they nevertheless directly affect interstate commerce.

(e) It is the purpose of this subchapter to eliminate abusive debt collection practices by debt collectors, to insure that those debt collectors who refrain from using abusive debt collection practices are not competitively disadvantaged, and to promote consistent State action to protect consumers against debt collection abuses.

§ 1692a. Definitions

"As used in this subchapter—

"(1) The term 'Commission' means the Federal Trade Commission.

"(2) The term 'communication' means the conveying of information regarding a debt directly or indirectly to any person through any medium.

"(3) The term 'consumer' means any natural person obligated or allegedly obligated to pay any debt.

" (4) The term 'creditor' means any person who offers or extends credit creating a debt or to whom a debt is owed, but such term does not include any person to the extent that he receives an assignment or transfer of a debt in default solely for the purpose of facilitating collection of such debt for another.

"(5) The term 'debt' means any obligation or alleged obligation of a consumer to pay money arising out of a transaction in which the money, property, insurance, or services which are the subject of the transaction are primarily for personal, family, or household purposes, whether or not such obligation has been reduced to judgment.

"(6) The term 'debt collector' means any person who uses any instrumentality of interstate commerce or the mails in any business the principal purpose of which is the collection of any debts, or who regularly collects or attempts to collect, directly or indirectly, debts owed or due or asserted to be owed or due another. Notwithstanding the exclusion provided by clause (G) of the last sentence of this paragraph, the term includes any creditor who, in the process of collecting his own debts, uses any name other than his own which would indicate that a third person is collecting or attempting to collect such debts. For the purpose of section 1692f(6) of this title, such term also includes any person who uses any instrumentality of interstate commerce or the mails in any business the principal purpose of which is the enforcement of security interests. The term does not include—

"(A) any officer or employee of a creditor while, in the name of the creditor, collecting debts for such creditor;

"(B) any person while acting as a debt collector for another person, both of whom are related by common ownership or affiliated by corporate control, if the person acting as a debt collector does so only for persons to whom it is so related or affiliated and if the principal business of such person is not the collection of debts;

"(C) any officer or employee of the United States or any State to the extent that collecting or attempting to collect any debt is in the performance of his official duties;

"(D) any person while serving or attempting to serve legal process on any other person in connection with the judicial enforcement of any debt;

"(E) any nonprofit organization which, at the request of consumers, performs bona fide consumer credit counseling and assists consumers in the liquidation of their debts by receiving payments from such consumers and distributing such amounts to creditor;

"(F) any attorney-at-law collecting a debt as an attorney on behalf of and in the name of a client; and

"(G) any person collecting or attempting to collect any debt owed or due or asserted to be owed or due another to the extent such activity (i) is incidental to a bona fide fiduciary obligation or a bona fide escrow arrangement; (ii) concerns a debt which was originated by such person; (iii) concerns a debt which was not in default at the time it was obtained by such person; or (iv) concerns a debt obtained by such person as a secured party in a commercial credit transaction involving the creditor.

"(7) The term 'location information' means a consumer's place of abode and his telephone number at such place, or his place of employment.

"(8) The term 'State' means any State, territory, or possession of the United States, the District of Columbia, the Commonwealth of Puerto Rico, or any political subdivision of any of the foregoing.

" § 1692b. Acquisition of location information

"Any debt collector communicating with any person other than the consumer for the purpose of acquiring location information about the consumer shall—

"(1) identify himself, state that he is confirming or correcting location information concerning the consumer, and, only if expressly requested, identify his employer;

"(2) not state that such consumer owes any debt;

"(3) not communicate with any such person more than once unless requested to do so by such person or unless the debt collector reasonably believes that the earlier response of such person is erroneous or incomplete and that such person now has correct or complete location information;

"(4) not communicate by post card;

"(5) not use any language or symbol on any envelope or in the contents of any communication effected by the mails or telegram that indicates that the debt collector is in the debt collection business or that the communication relates to the collection of a debt; and

"(6) after the debt collector knows the consumer is represented by an attorney with regard to the subject debt and has knowledge of, or can readily ascertain, such attorney's name and address, not communicate with any person other than that attorney, unless the attorney fails to respond within a reasonable period of time to communication from the debt collector.

" § 1692c. Communication in connection with debt collection

"(a) *Communication with the consumer generally*—Without the prior consent of the consumer given directly to the debt collector or the express permission of a court of competent jurisdiction, a debt collector may not communicate with a consumer in connection with the collection of any debt—

"(1) at any unusual time or place or a time or place known or which should be known to be inconvenient to the consumer. In the absence of knowledge of circumstances to the contrary, a debt collector shall assume that the convenient time for communicating with a consumer is after 8 o'clock antemeridian and before 9 o'clock postmeridian, local time at the consumer's location;

"(2) if the debt collector knows the consumer is represented by an attorney with respect to such debt and has knowledge of, or can readily ascertain, such attorney's name and address, unless the attorney fails to respond within a reasonable period of time to a communication from the debt collector or unless the attorney consents to direct communication with the consumer; or

"(3) at the consumer's place of employment if the debt collector knows or has reason to know that the consumer's employer prohibits the consumer from receiving such communication.

"(b) *Communication with third parties*—Except as provided in section 1692b of this title, without the prior consent of the consumer given directly to the debt collector, or the express permission of a court of competent jurisdiction, or as reasonably necessary to effectuate a post-judgment judicial remedy, a debt collector may not communicate, in connection with the collection of any debt, with any person other than the consumer, his attorney, a consumer reporting agency if otherwise permitted by law, the creditor, the attorney of the creditor, or the attorney of the debt collector.

"(c) *Ceasing communication*—If a consumer notifies a debt collector in writing that the consumer refuses to pay a debt or that the consumer wishes the debt collector to cease further communication with the consumer, the debt collector shall not communicate further with the consumer with respect to such debt, except—

"(1) to advise the consumer that the debt collector's further efforts are being terminated;

"(2) to notify the consumer that the debt collector or creditor may invoke specified remedies which are ordinarily invoked by such debt collector or creditor; or

"(3) where applicable, to notify the consumer that the debt collector or creditor intends to invoke a specified remedy.

"If such notice from the consumer is made by mail, notification shall be complete upon receipt.

"(d) *Definitions*—For the purpose of this section, the term 'consumer' includes the consumer's spouse, parent (if the consumer is a minor), guardian, executor, or administrator.

" § 1692d. Harassment or abuse

"A debt collector may not engage in any conduct the natural consequence of which is to harass, oppress, or abuse any person in connection with the collection of a debt. Without limiting the general application of the foregoing, the following conduct is a violation of this section:

"(1) The use or threat of use of violence or other criminal means to harm the physical person, reputation, or property of any person.

"(2) The use of obscene or profane language or language the natural consequence of which is to abuse the hearer or reader.

"(3) The publication of a list of consumers who allegedly refuse to pay debts, except to a consumer reporting agency or to persons meeting the requirements of section 1681a(f) or 1681b(3) of this title.

"(4) The advertisement for sale of any debt to coerce payment of the debt.

"(5) Causing a telephone to ring or engaging any person in telephone conversation repeatedly or continuously with intent to annoy, abuse, or harass any person at the called number.

"(6) Except as provided in section 1692b of this title, the placement of telephone calls without meaningful disclosure of the caller's identity.

" § 1692e. False or misleading representations

"A debt collector may not use any false, deceptive, or misleading representation or means in connection with the collection of any debt. Without limiting the general application of the foregoing, the following conduct is a violation of this section:

"(1) The false representation or implication that the debt collector is vouched for, bonded by, or affiliated with the United States or any State, including the use of any badge, uniform, or facsimile thereof.

"(2) The false representation of—

"(A) the character, amount, or legal status of any debt; or

"(B) any services rendered or compensation which may be lawfully received by any debt collector for the collection of a debt.

"(3) The false representation or implication that any individual is an attorney or that any communication is from an attorney.

"(4) The representation or implication that nonpayment of any debt will result in the arrest or imprisonment of any person or the seizure, garnishment, attachment, or sale of any property or wages of any person unless such action is lawful and the debt collector or creditor intends to take such action.

"(5) The threat to take any action that cannot legally be taken or that is not intended to be taken.

"(6) The false representation or implication that a sale, referral, or other transfer of any interest in a debt shall cause the consumer to—

"(A) lose any claim or defense to payment of the debt; or

"(B) become subject to any practice prohibited by this subchapter.

"(7) The false representation or implication that the consumer committed any crime or other conduct in order to disgrace the consumer.

"(8) Communicating or threatening to communicate to any person credit information which is known or which should be known to be false, including the failure to communicate that a disputed debt is disputed.

"(9) The use or distribution of any written communication which simulates or is falsely represented to be a document authorized, issued, or approved by any court, official, or agency of the United States or any State, or which creates a false impression as to its source, authorization, or approval.

"(10) The use of any false representation or deceptive means to collect or attempt to collect any debt or to obtain information concerning a consumer.

"(11) Except as otherwise provided for communications to acquire location information under section 1692b of this title, the failure to disclose clearly in all communications made to collect a debt or to obtain information about a consumer, that the debt collector is attempting to collect a debt and that any information obtained will be used for that purpose.

"(12) The false representation or implication that accounts have been turned over to innocent purchasers for value.

"(13) The false representation or implication that documents are legal process.

"(14) The use of any business, company, or organization name other than the true name of the debt collector's business, company, or organization.

"(15) The false representation or implication that documents are not legal process forms or do not require action by the consumer.

"(16) The false representation or implication that a debt collector operates or is employed by a consumer reporting agency as defined by section 1681a(f) of this title.

" § 1692f. Unfair practices

"A debt collector may not use unfair or unconscionable means to collect or attempt to collect any debt. Without limiting the general application of the foregoing, the following conduct is a violation of this section:

"(1) The collection of any amount (including any interest, fee, charge, or expense incidental to the principal obligation) unless such amount is expressly authorized by the agreement creating the debt or permitted by law.

"(2) The acceptance by a debt collector from any person of a check or other payment instrument postdated by more than five days unless such person is notified in writing of the debt collector's intent to deposit such check or instrument not more than ten nor less than three business days prior to such deposit.

"(3) The solicitation by a debt collector of any postdated check or other postdated payment instrument for the purpose of threatening or instituting criminal prosecution.

"(4) Depositing or threatening to deposit any postdated check or other postdated payment instrument prior to the date on such check or instrument.

"(5) Causing charges to be made to any person for communications by concealment of the true purpose of the communication. Such charges include, but are not limited to, collect telephone calls and telegram fees.

"(6) Taking or threatening to take any nonjudicial action to effect dispossession or disablement of property if—

"(A) there is no present right to possession of the property claimed as collateral through an enforceable security interest;

"(B) there is no present intention to take possession of the property; or

"(C) the property is exempt by law from such dispossession or disablement.

"(7) Communicating with a consumer regarding a debt by post card.

"(8) Using any language or symbol, other than the debt collector's address, on any envelope when communicating with a consumer by use of the mails or by telegram, except that a debt collector may use his business name if such name does not indicate that he is in the debt collection business.

" § 1692g. Validation of debts

"Notice of debt; contents

"(a) Within five days after the initial communication with a consumer in connection with the collection of any debt, a debt collector shall, unless the following information is contained in the initial communication or the consumer has paid the debt, send the consumer a written notice containing—

"(1) the amount of the debt;

"(2) the name of the creditor to whom the debt is owed;

"(3) a statement that unless the consumer, within thirty days after receipt of the notice, disputes the validity of the debt, or any portion thereof, the debt will be assumed to be valid by the debt collector;

"(4) a statement that if the consumer notifies the debt collector in writing within the thirty-day period that the debt, or any portion thereof, is disputed, the debt collector will obtain verification of the debt or a copy of a judgment against the consumer and a copy of such verification or judgment will be mailed to the consumer by the debt collector; and

"(5) a statement that, upon the consumer's written request within the thirty-day period, the debt collector will provide the consumer with the name and address of the original creditor, if different from the current creditor.

"Disputed debts

"(b) If the consumer notifies the debt collector in writing within the thirty-day period described in subsection (a) of this section that the debt, or any portion thereof, is disputed, or that the consumer requests the name and address of the original creditor, the debt collector shall cease collection of the debt, or any portion thereof, until the debt collector obtains verification of the debt or a copy of a judgment, or the name and address of the original creditor, and a copy of such verification or judgment, or name and address of the original creditor, is mailed to the consumer by the debt collector.

"Admission of liability

"(c) The failure of a consumer to dispute the validity of a debt under this section may not be construed by any court as an admission of liability by the consumer.

" § 1692h. Multiple debts

"If any consumer owes multiple debts and makes any single payment to any debt collector with respect to such debts, such debt collector may not apply such payment to any debt which is disputed by the consumer and, where applicable, shall apply such payment in accordance with the consumer's directions.

" § 1692i. Legal actions by debt collectors

"(a) Any debt collector who brings any legal action on a debt against any consumer shall—

"(1) in the case of an action to enforce an interest in real property securing the consumer's obligation, bring such action only in a judicial district or similar legal entity in which such real property is located; or

"(2) in the case of an action not described in paragraph (1), bring such action only in the judicial district or similar legal entity—

"(A) in which such consumer signed the contract sued upon; or

"(B) in which such consumer resides at the commencement of the action.

"(b) Nothing in this subchapter shall be construed to authorize the bringing of legal actions by debt collectors.

" § 1692j. Furnishing certain deceptive forms

"(a) It is unlawful to design, compile, and furnish any form knowing that such form would be used to create the false belief in a consumer that a person other than the creditor of such consumer is participating in the collection of or in an attempt to collect a debt such consumer allegedly owes such creditor, when in fact such person is not so participating.

"(b) Any person who violates this section shall be liable to the same extent and in the same manner as a debt collector is liable under section 1692k of this title for failure to comply with a provision of this subchapter.

" § 1692k. Civil liability

"Amount of damages

"(a) Except as otherwise provided by this section, any debt collector who fails to comply with any provision of this subchapter with respect to any person is liable to such person in an amount equal to the sum of—

"(1) any actual damage sustained by such person as a result of such failure;

"(2) (A) in the case of any action by an individual, such additional damages as the court may allow, but not exceeding $1,000; or

"(B) in the case of a class action, (i) such amount for each named plaintiff as could be recovered under subparagraph (A), and (ii) such amount as the court may allow for all other class members, without regard to a minimum individual recovery, not to exceed the lesser of $500,000 or 1 per centum of the net worth of the debt collector; and

"(3) in the case of any successful action to enforce the foregoing liability, the costs of the action, together with a reasonable attorney's fee as determined by the court. On a finding by the court that an action under this section was brought in bad faith and for the purpose of harassment, the court may award to the defendant attorney's fees reasonable in relation to the work expended and costs.

"Factors considered by court

"(b) In determining the amount of liability in any action under subsection (a) of this section, the court shall consider, among other relevant factors—

"(1) in any individual action under subsection (a)(2)(A) of this section, the frequency and persistence of noncompliance by the debt collector, the nature of such noncompliance, and the extent to which such noncompliance was intentional; or

"(2) in any class action under subsection (a)(2)(B) of this section, the frequency and persistence of noncompliance by the debt collector, the nature of such noncompliance, the resources of the debt collector, the number of persons adversely affected, and the extent to which the debt collector's noncompliance was intentional.

"Intent

"(c) A debt collector may not be held liable in any action brought under this subchapter if the debt collector shows by a preponderance of evidence that the violation was not intentional and resulted from a bona fide error notwithstanding the maintenance of procedures reasonably adapted to avoid any such error.

"Jurisdiction

"(d) An action to enforce any liability created by this subchapter may be brought in any appropriate United States district court without regard to the amount in controversy, or in any other court of competent jurisdiction, within one year from the date on which the violation occurs.

"Advisory opinions of Commission

"(e) No provision of this section imposing any liability shall apply to any act done or omitted in good faith in confor-

mity with any advisory opinion of the Commission, notwithstanding that after such act or omission has occurred, such opinion is amended, rescinded, or determined by judicial or other authority to be invalid for any reason."

FAIR CREDIT BILLING ACT (FCBA)

The FCBA is key to many of the disputes in this book, because it puts a burden on many creditors to bill you in a certain manner before a debt can be considered late. In many situations, it protects you from being considered late in payment if you contest part of a bill.

"Title III—Fair Credit Billing

"Sec. 301. Short title

"This title may be cited as the 'Fair Credit Billing Act.'

"Sec. 302. Declaration of purpose

"The last sentence of section 102 of the Truth in Lending Act (15 U.S.C. 1601) is amended by striking out the period and inserting in lieu thereof a comma and the following: 'and to protect the consumer against inaccurate and unfair credit billing and credit card practices.'

"Sec. 303. Definitions of creditor and open end credit plan

"The first sentence of section 103 (f) of the Truth in Lending Act (15 U.S.C. 1602) (f) is amended to read as follows: 'The term "creditor" refers only to creditors who regularly extend, or arrange for the extension of, credit which is payable by agreement in more than four installments or for which the payment of a finance charge is or may be required, whether in connection with loans, sales of property or services, or otherwise. For the purposes of the requirements imposed under Chapter 4 and sections 127 (a)(6), 127 (a)(7), 127 (a)(8), 127 (b)(1), 127 (b)(2), 127 (b)(3), 127 (b)(9), and 127 (b)(11) of Chapter 2 of this Title, the term "creditor" shall also include card issuers whether or not the amount due is payable by agreement in more than four installments or the payment of a finance charge is or may be required, and the Board shall, by regulation, apply these requirements to such card issuers, to the extent appropriate, even though the requirements are by their terms applicable only to creditors offering open end credit plans.'

"Sec. 304. Disclosure of fair credit billing rights

"(a) Section 127 (a) of the Truth in Lending Act (15 U.S.C. 1637 (a)) is amended by adding at the end thereof a new paragraph as follows:

" '(8) A statement, in a form prescribed by regulations of the Board of the protection provided by sections 161 and 170 to an obligor and the creditor's responsibilities under sections 162 and 170. With respect to each of two billing cycles per year, at semiannual intervals, the creditor shall transmit such statement to each obligor to whom the creditor is required to transmit a statement pursuant to section 127 (b) for such billing cycle.'

"(b) Section 127 (c) of such Act (15 U.S.C. 1637 (c)) is amended to read:

" '(c) In the case of any existing account under an open end consumer credit plan having an outstanding balance of more than $1 at or after the close of the creditor's first full billing cycle under the plan after the effective date of subsection (a) or any amendments thereto, the items described in subsection (a), to the extent applicable and not previously disclosed, shall be disclosed in a notice mailed or delivered to the obligor not later than the time of mailing the next statement required by subsection (b).'

"Sec. 305. Disclosure of billing contact

"Section 127 (b) of the Truth in Lending Act (15 U.S.C. 1637 (b)) is amended by adding at the end thereof a new paragraph as follows:

" '(11) The address to be used by the creditor for the purpose of receiving billing inquiries from the obligor.'

"Sec. 306. Billing practices

"The Truth in Lending Act (15 U.S.C. 1601–1665) is amended by adding at the end thereof a new chapter as follows:

" 'Chapter 4—Credit Billing'

"Sec. 161. Correction of billing errors

"(a) If a creditor, within sixty days after having transmitted to an obligor a statement of the obligor's account in connection with an extension of consumer credit, receives at the address disclosed under section 127 (b)(11) a written notice (other than notice on a payment stub or other payment medium supplied by the creditor if the creditor so stipulates with the disclosure required under section 127 (a)(8) from the obligor in which the obligor—

"(1) sets forth or otherwise enables the creditor to identify the name and account number (if any) of the obligor,

"(2) indicates the obligor's belief that the statement contains a billing error and the amount of such billing error, and

"(3) sets forth the reasons for the obligor's belief (to the extent applicable) that the statement contains a billing error, the creditor shall, unless the obligor has, after giving such written notice and before the expiration of the time limits herein specified, agreed that the statement was correct—

"(A) not later than thirty days after

the receipt of the notice, send a written acknowledgement thereof to the obligor, unless the action required in subparagraph (B) is taken within such thirty-day period, and

"(B) not later than two complete billing cycles of the creditor (in no event later than ninety days) after the receipt of the notice and prior to taking any action to collect the amount, or any part thereof, indicated by the obligor under paragraph (2) either—

"(i) make appropriate corrections in the account of this obligor, including the crediting of any finance charges on amounts erroneously billed, and transmit to the obligor a notification of such corrections and the creditor's explanation of any change in the amount indicated by the obligor under paragraph (2) and, if any such change is made and the obligor so requests, copies of documentary evidence of the obligor's indebtedness; or

"(ii) send a written explanation or clarification to the obligor, after having conducted an investigation, setting forth to the extent applicable the reasons why the creditor believes the account of the obligor was correctly shown in the statement and, upon request of the obligor, provide copies of documentary evidence of the obligor's indebtedness. In the case of a billing error where the obligor alleges that the creditor's billing statement reflects goods not delivered to the obligor or his designee in accordance with the agreement made at the time of the transaction, a creditor may not construe such amount to be correctly shown unless he determines that such goods were actually delivered, mailed, or otherwise sent to the obligor and provides the obligor with a statement of such determination.

"After complying with the provisions of this subsection with respect to an alleged billing error, a creditor has no further responsibility under this section if the obligor continues to make substantially the same allegation with respect to such error.

"(b) For the purpose of this section, a 'billing error' consists of any of the following:

"(1) A reflection on a statement of an extension of credit which was not made to the obligor or, if made, was not in the amount reflected on such statement.

"(2) A reflection on a statement of an extension of credit for which the obligor requests additional clarification including documentary evidence thereof.

"(3) A reflection on a statement of goods or services not accepted by the obligor or his designee or not delivered to the obligor or his designee in accordance with the agreement made at the time of a transaction.

"(4) The creditor's failure to reflect properly on a statement a payment made by the obligor or a credit issued to the obligor.

"(5) A computation error or similar error of an accounting nature of the creditor on a statement.

"(6) Any other error described in regulations of the Board.

"(c) For the purposes of this section, 'action to collect the amount,' or any part thereof, indicated by an obligor under paragraph (2) does not include the sending of statements of account to the obligor following written notice from the obligor as specified under subsection (a), if—

"(1) the obligor's account is not restricted or closed because of the failure of the obligor to pay the amount indicated under paragraph (2) of subsection (a), and

"(2) the creditor indicates the payment of such amount is not required pending the creditor's compliance with this section.

"Nothing in this section shall be construed to prohibit any action by a creditor to collect any amount which has not been indicated by the obligor to contain a billing error.

"(d) Pursuant to regulations of the Board, a creditor operating an open end consumer credit plan may not, prior to the sending of the written explanation or clarification required under paragraph (B) (ii), restrict or close an account with respect to which the obligor has indicated pursuant to subsection (a) that he believes such account to contain a billing error solely because of the obligor's failure to pay the amount indicated to be in error. Nothing in this subsection shall be deemed to prohibit a creditor from applying against the credit limit on the obligor's account the amount indicated to be in error.

"(e) Any creditor who fails to comply with the requirements of this section or section 162 forfeits any right to collect from the obligor the amount indicated by the obligor under paragraph (2) of subsection (a) of this section, and any finance charges thereon, except that the amount required to be forfeited under this subsection may not exceed $50.

"Sec. 162. Regulation of credit reports

"(a) After receiving a notice from an obligor as provided in section 161 (a), a creditor or his agent may not directly or indirectly threaten to report to any person adversely on the obligor's credit rating or credit standing because of the obligor's failure to pay the amount indicated by the obligor under section 161 (a)(2), and such amount may not be reported as delinquent to any third party until the creditor has met the requirements of section 161 and has allowed the obligor the same number of days (not less than ten) thereafter to make payment as is provided under the credit agreement with the obligor for the payment of undisputed amounts.

"(b) If a creditor receives a further written notice from an obligor that an amount is still in dispute within the time allowed for payment under subsection (a) of this section, a creditor may not report to any third party that the amount of the obligor is delinquent because the obligor has failed to pay an amount which he has indicated under section 161 (a)(2), unless the creditor also reports that the amount is in dispute and, at the same time, notifies the obligor of the name and address of each party to whom the creditor is reporting information concerning the delinquency.

"(c) A creditor shall report any subsequent resolution of any delinquencies reported pursuant to subsection (b) to the parties to whom such delinquencies were initially reported.

"Sec. 163. Length of billing period

"(a) If an open end consumer credit plan provides a time period within which an obligor may repay any portion of the credit extended without incurring an additional finance charge, such additional finance charge may not be imposed with respect to such portion of the credit extended for the billing cycle of which such period is a part unless a statement which includes the amount upon which the finance charge for that period is based was mailed at least fourteen days prior to the date specified in the statement by which payment must be made in order to avoid imposition of that finance charge.

"(b) Subsection (a) does not apply in any case where a creditor has been prevented, delayed, or hindered in making timely mailing or delivery of such periodic statement within the time period specified in such subsection because of an act of God, war, natural disaster, strike, or other excusable or justifiable cause, as determined under regulations of the Board.

"Sec. 164. Prompt crediting of payments

"Payments received from an obligor under an open end consumer credit plan by the creditor shall be posted promptly to the obligor's account as specified in regulations of the Board. Such regulations shall prevent a finance charge from being imposed on any obligor if the creditor has received the obligor's payment in readily identifiable form in the amount, manner, location, and time indicated by the credit to avoid the imposition thereof.

"Sec. 165. Crediting excess payments

"Whenever an obligor transmits funds to a creditor in excess of the total balance due on an open end consumer credit account, the creditor shall promptly (1) upon request of the obligor refund the amount of the overpayment, or (2) credit such amount to the obligor's account.

"Sec. 166. Prompt notification of returns

"With respect to any sales transaction where a credit card has been used to obtain credit, where the seller is a person other than the card issuer, and where the seller accepts or allows a return of the goods or forgiveness of a debit for services which were the subject of such sale, the seller shall promptly transmit to the credit card issuer, a credit statement with respect thereto and the credit card issuer shall credit the account of the obligor for the amount of the transaction.

"Sec. 167. Use of cash discounts

"(a) With respect to credit card which may be used for extensions of credit in sales transactions in which the seller is a person other than the card issuer; the card issuer may not, by contract or oth-

erwise, prohibit any such seller from offering a discount to a cardholder to induce the cardholder to pay by cash, check, or similar means rather than use a credit card.

"(b) With respect to any sales transaction, and discount not in excess of 5 per centum offered by the seller for the purpose of inducing payment by cash, check, or other means not involving the use of a credit card shall not constitute a finance charge as determined under section 106, if such discount is offered to all prospective buyers and its availability is disclosed to all prospective buyers clearly and conspicuously in accordance with regulations of the Board.

"Sec. 168. Prohibition of tie-in services

"Notwithstanding any agreement to the contrary, a card issuer may not require a seller, as a condition to participating in a credit card plan, to open an account with or procure any other service from the card issuer or its subsidiary or agent.

"Sec. 169. Prohibition of offsets

"(a) A card issuer may not take any action to offset a cardholder's indebtedness arising in connection with a consumer credit transaction under the relevant credit card plan against funds of the cardholder held on deposit with the card issuer unless—

"(1) such action was previously authorized in writing by the cardholder in accordance with a credit plan whereby the cardholder agrees periodically to pay debts incurred in his open end credit account by permitting the card issuer periodically to deduct all or a portion of such debt from the cardholder's deposit account, and

"(2) such action with respect to any outstanding disputed amount not be taken by the card issuer upon request of the cardholder. In the case of any credit card account in existence on the effective date of this section, the previous written authorization referred to in clause (1) shall not be required until the date (after such effective date) when such account is renewed, but in no case later than one year after such effective date. Such written authorization shall be deemed to exist if the card issuer has previously notified the cardholder that the use of his credit card account will subject any funds which the card issuer holds in deposit accounts of such cardholder to offset against any amounts due and payable on his credit card account which have not been paid in accordance with the terms of the agreement between the card issuer and the cardholder.

"(b) This section does not alter or affect the right under State law of a card issuer to attach or otherwise levy upon funds of a cardholder held on deposit with the card issuer if that remedy is constitutionally available to creditors generally.

"Sec. 170. Rights of credit card customers

"(a) Subject to the limitation contained in subsection (b), a card issuer who has issued a credit card to a cardholder pursuant to an open end consumer credit plan shall be subject to all claims (other than tort claims) and defenses arising out of any transaction in which the credit card is used as a method of payment or extension of credit if (1) the obligor has made a good faith attempt to obtain satisfactory resolution of a disagreement or problem relative to the transaction from the person honoring the credit card; (2) the amount of the initial transaction exceeds $50; and (3) the place where the initial transaction occurred was in the same State as the mailing address previously provided by the cardholder or was within 100 miles

from such address, except that the limitations set forth in clauses (2) and (3) with respect to an obligor's right to asset claims and defenses against a card issuer shall not be applicable to any transaction in which the person honoring the credit card (A) is the same person as the card issuer, (B) is controlled by the card issuer, (C) is under direct or indirect common control with the card issuer, (D) is a franchised dealer in the card issuer's products or services, or (E) has obtained the order for such transaction through a mail solicitation made by or participated in by the card issuer in which the cardholder is solicited to enter into such transaction by using the credit card issued by the card issuer.

"(b) The amount of claims or defenses asserted by the cardholder may not exceed the amount of credit outstanding with respect to such transaction at the time the cardholder first notifies the card issuer or the person honoring the credit card of such claim or defense. For the purpose of determining the amount of credit outstanding in the preceding sentence, payments and credits to the cardholder's account are deemed to have been applied, in the order indicated, to the payment of: (1) late charges in the order of their entry to the account; (2) finance charges in order of their entry to the account; and (3) debits to the account other than those set forth above, in the order in which each debit entry to the account was made.

"Sec. 171. Relation to State laws

"(a) This chapter does not annul, alter, or affect, or exempt any person subject to the provisions of this chapter from complying with, the laws of any State with respect to credit billing practices, except to the extent that those laws are inconsistent with any provision of this chapter, and then only to the extent of the inconsistency. The Board may not determine that any State law is inconsistent with any provision of this chapter if the Board determines that such law gives greater protection to the consumer.

"(b) The Board shall by regulation exempt from the requirements of this chapter any class of credit transactions within any State if it determines that under the law of that State that class of transactions is subject to requirements substantially similar to those imposed under this chapter or that such law gives greater protection to the consumer, and that there is adequate provision for enforcement."

TRUTH IN LENDING ACT (TILA)

The TILA helps spell out consumer rights in mortgages and leases. Truth in lending focuses on issues such as finance charges, fees, and surcharges to credit transactions, as well as mandatory disclosures and consumers rights to break contracts within three days of signing. The act also covers the issue of payment deadlines and can therefore be useful in making an argument about the relative lateness of payment with regard to a loan agreement.

"Consumer Credit Protection Act

"Public Law 90–321; 82 Stat. 146
"An Act to safeguard the consumer in connection with the utilization of credit by requiring full disclosure of the terms and conditions of finance charges in credit transactions or in offers to extend credit; by restricting the garnishment of wages; and by creating the National Commission on Consumer Finance to study and make recommendations on the need for further regulation of the consumer finance industry; and for other purposes.

"Be it enacted by the Senate and House of Representatives of the United States of America in Congress assembled, That:
"Sec. 1. Short title of entire Act
"This Act may be cited as the Consumer Credit Protection Act.

"Title I—Consumer Credit Cost Disclosure

"Chapter
"1. GENERAL PROVISIONS   101
"2. CREDIT TRANSACTIONS 121
"3. CREDIT ADVERTISING   141

"Chapter 1—General Provisions

"Sec. 101. Short title
This title may be cited as the Truth in Lending Act.

"Sec. 102. Findings and declaration of purpose
"The Congress finds that economic stabilization would be enhanced and the competition among the various financial institutions and other firms engaged in the extension of consumer credit would be strengthened by the informed use of credit. The informed use of credit results from an awareness of the cost thereof by consumers. It is the purpose of this title to assure a meaningful disclosure of credit terms so that the consumer will be able to compare more readily the various credit terms available to him and avoid the uninformed use of credit.

"Sec. 103. Definitions and rules of construction
"(a) The definitions and rules of construction set forth in this section are applicable for the purposes of this title.

"(b) The term 'Board' refers to the Board of Governors of the Federal Reserve System.

"(c) The term 'organization' means a corporation, government or governmental subdivision or agency, trust, estate, partnership, cooperative, or association.

"(d) The term 'person' means a natural person or an organization.

"(e) The term 'credit' means the right granted by a creditor to a debtor to defer payment of debt or to incur debt and defer its payment.

"(f) The term 'creditor' refers only to creditors who regularly extend, or arrange for the extension of, credit for which the payment of a finance charge is required, whether in connection with loans, sales of property or services, or otherwise. The provisions of this title apply to any such creditor, irrespective of his or its status as a natural person or any type of organization.

"(g) The term 'credit sale' refers to any sale with respect to which credit is extended or arranged by the seller. The term includes any contract in the form of a bailment or lease if the bailee or lessee contracts to pay as compensation for use a sum substantially equivalent to or in excess of the aggregate value of the property and services involved and it is agreed that the bailee or lessee will become, or for no other or a nominal consideration has the option to become, the owner of the property upon full compliance with his obligations under the contract.

"(h) The adjective 'consumer,' used with reference to a credit transaction, characterizes the transaction as one in which the party to whom credit is offered or extended is a natural person, and the money, property, or services which are the subject of the transaction are primarily for personal, family, household, or agricultural purposes.

"(i) The term 'open end credit plan' refers to a plan prescribing the terms of credit transactions which may be made

thereunder from time to time and under the terms of which a finance charge may be computed on the outstanding unpaid balance from time to time thereunder.

"(j) The term 'State' refers to any State, the Commonwealth of Puerto Rico, the District of Columbia, and any territory or possession of the United States.

"(k) Any reference to any requirement imposed under this title or any provision thereof includes reference to the regulations of the Board under this title or the provision thereof in question.

"(l) The disclosure of an amount or percentage which is greater than the amount or percentage required to be disclosed under this title does not in itself constitute a violation of this title.

"Sec. 104. Exempted transactions

"This title does not apply to the following:

"(1) Credit transactions involving extensions of credit for business or commercial purposes, or to government or governmental agencies or instrumentalities, or to organizations.

"(2) Transactions in securities or commodities accounts by a broker-dealer registered with the Securities and Exchange Commission.

"(3) Credit transactions, other than real property transactions, in which the total amount to be financed exceeds $25,000.

"(4) Transactions under public utility tariffs, if the Board determines that a State regulatory body regulates the charges for the public utility services involved, the charges for delayed payment, and any discount allowed for early payment.

"Sec. 105. Regulations

"The Board shall prescribe regulations to carry out the purposes of this title. These regulations may contain such classifications, differentiations, or other provisions, and may provide for such adjustments and exceptions for any class of transactions, as in the judgment of the Board are necessary or proper to effectuate the purposes of this title, to prevent circumvention or evasion thereof, or to facilitate compliance therewith.

"Sec. 106. Determination of finance charge

"(a) Except as otherwise provided in this section, the amount of the finance charge in connection with any consumer credit transaction shall be determined as the sum of all charges, payable directly or indirectly by the person to whom the credit is extended, and imposed directly or indirectly by the creditor as an incident to the extension of credit, including any of the following types of charges which are applicable:

"(1) Interest, time price differential, and any amount payable under a point, discount, or other system of additional charges.

"(2) Service or carrying charge.

"(3) Loan fee, finder's fee, or similar charge.

"(4) Fee for an investigation or credit report.

"(5) Premium or other charge for any guarantee or insurance protecting the creditor against the obligor's default or other credit loss.

"(b) Charges or premiums for credit life, accident, or health insurance written in connection with any consumer credit transaction shall be included in the finance charge unless

"(1) the coverage of the debtor by the insurance is not a factor in the approval by the creditor of the extension of credit, and this fact is clearly disclosed in writing to the person applying for or obtaining the extension of credit; and

"(2) in order to obtain the insurance in connection with the extension of credit, the person to whom the credit is extended must give specific affirmative written indication of his desire to do so after written disclosure to him of the cost thereof.

"(c) Charges or premiums for insurance, written in connection with any consumer credit transaction, against loss of or damage to property or against liability arising out of the ownership or use of property, shall be included in the finance charge unless a clear and specific statement in writing is furnished by the creditor to the person to whom the credit is extended, setting forth the cost of the insurance if obtained from or through the creditor, and stating that the person to whom the credit is extended may choose the person through which the insurance is to be obtained.

"(d) If any of the following items is itemized and disclosed in accordance with the regulations of the Board in connection with any transaction, then the creditor need not include that item in the computation of the finance charge with respect to that transaction:

"(1) Fees and charges prescribed by law which actually are or will be paid to public officials for determining the existence of or for perfecting or releasing or satisfying any security related to the credit transaction.

"(2) The premium payable for an insurance in lieu of perfecting any security interest otherwise required by the creditor in connection with the transaction, if the premium does not exceed the fees and charges described in paragraph (1) which would otherwise be payable.

"(3) Taxes.

"(4) Any other type of charge which is not for credit and the exclusion of which from the finance charge is approved by the Board by regulation.

"(e) The following items, when

charged in connection with any extension of credit secured by an interest in real property, shall not be included in the computation of the finance charge with respect to that transaction:

"(1) Fees or premiums for title examination, title insurance, or similar purposes.

"(2) Fees for preparation of a deed, settlement statement, or other documents.

"(3) Escrows for future payments of taxes and insurance.

"(4) Fees for notarizing deeds and other documents.

"(5) Appraisal fees.

"(6) Credit reports.

"Sec. 107. Determination of annual percentage rate

"(a) The annual percentage rate applicable to any extension of consumer credit shall be determined, in accordance with the regulations of the Board,

"(1) in the case of any extension of credit other than under an open end credit plan, as

"(A) that nominal annual percentage rate which will yield a sum equal to the amount of the finance charge when it is applied to the unpaid balances of the amount financed, calculated according to the actuarial method of allocating payments made on a debt between the amount financed and the amount of the finance charge, pursuant to which a payment is applied first to the accumulated finance charge and the balance is applied to the unpaid amount financed; or

"(B) the rate determined by any method prescribed by the Board as a method which materially simplifies computation while retaining reasonable accuracy as compared with the rate determined under subparagraph (A).

"(2) in the case of any extension of credit under an open end credit plan, as

the quotient (expressed as a percentage) of the total finance charge for the period to which it relates divided by the amount upon which the finance charge for that period is based, multiplied by the number of such periods in a year.

"(b) Where a creditor imposes the same finance charge for balances within a specified range, the annual percentage rate shall be computed on the median balance within the range, except that if the Board determines that a rate so computed would not be meaningful, or would be materially misleading, the annual percentage rate shall be computed on such other basis as the Board may be regulation required.

"(c) The annual percentage rate may be rounded to the nearest quarter of 1 per centum for credit transactions payable in substantially equal installments when a creditor determines the total finance charge on the basis of a single add-on, discount, periodic, or other rate, and the rate is converted into an annual percentage rate under procedures prescribed by the Board.

"(d) The Board may authorize the use of rate tables or charts which may provide for the disclosure of annual percentage rates which vary from the rate determined in accordance with subsection (a) (1) (A) by not more than such tolerances as the Board may allow. The Board may not allow a tolerance greater than 8 per centum of that rate except to simplify compliance where irregular payments are involved.

"(e) In the case of creditors determining the annual percentage rate in a manner other than as described in subsection (c) or (d), the Board may authorize other reasonable tolerances.

"(f) Prior to January 1, 1971, any rate required under this title to be disclosed as a percentage rate may, at the option of the creditor, be expressed in the form of the corresponding ratio of dollars per hundred dollars.

"Sec. 108. Administrative enforcement

"(a) Compliance with the requirements imposed under this title shall be enforced under

"(1) section 8 of the Federal Deposit Insurance Act, in the case of

"(A) national banks, by the Comptroller of the Currency.

"(B) member banks of the Federal Reserve System (other than national banks), by the Board.

"(C) banks insured by the Federal Deposit Insurance Corporation (other than members of the Federal Reserve System), by the Board of Directors of the Federal Deposit Insurance Corporation.

"(2) section 5 (d) of the Home Owners' Loan Act of 1933, section 407 of the National Housing Act, and sections 6 (f) and 17 of the Federal Home Loan Bank Art, by the Federal Home Loan Bank Board (acting directly or through the Federal Savings and Loan Insurance Corporation), in the case of any institution subject to any of those provisions.

"(3) the Federal Credit Union Act, by the Director of the Bureau of Federal Credit Unions with respect to any Federal credit union.

"(4) the Acts to regulate commerce, by the Interstate Commerce Commission with respect to any common carrier subject to those Acts.

"(5) the Federal Aviation Act of 1958, by the Civil Aeronautics Board with respect to any air carrier or foreign air carrier subject to that Act.

"(6) the Packers and Stockyards Act, 1921 (except as provided in section 406 of that Act), by the Secretary of Agriculture with respect to any activities subject to that Act.

"(b) For the Purpose of the Exercise by any agency referred to in subsection (a) of its powers under any Act referred to in that subsection, a violation of any requirement imposed under this title shall be deemed to be a violation of a requirement imposed under that Act. In addition to its powers under any provision of law specifically referred to in subsection (a), each of the agencies referred to in that subsection may exercise, for the purpose of enforcing compliance with any requirement imposed under this title, any other authority conferred on it by law.

"(c) Except to the extent that enforcement of the requirements imposed under this title is specifically committed to some other Government agency under subsection (a), the Federal Trade Commission shall enforce such requirements. For the purpose of the exercise by the Federal Trade Commission of its functions and powers under the Federal Trade Commission Act, a violation of any requirement imposed under that Act. All of the functions and powers of the Federal Trade Commission under the Federal Trade Commission Act are available to the Commission to enforce compliance by any person with the requirements imposed under this title, irrespective of whether that person is engaged in commerce or meets any other jurisdictional tests in the Federal Trade Commission Act.

"(d) The authority of the Board to issue regulations under this title does not impair the authority of any other agency designated in this section to make rules respecting its own procedures in enforcing compliance with requirements imposed under this title.

"Sec. 109. Views of other agencies

"In the exercise of its functions under this title, the Board may obtain upon request the views of any other Federal agency which, in the judgment of the Board, exercises regulatory or supervisory functions with respect to any class of creditors subject to this title.

"Sec. 110. Advisory committee

"The Board shall establish an advisory committee to advise and consult with it in the exercise of its functions under this title. In appointing the members of the committee, the Board shall seek to achieve a fair representation of the interests of sellers of merchandise on credit, lenders, and the public. The committee shall meet from time to time at the call of the Board, and members thereof shall be paid transportation expenses not to exceed $100 per diem.

"Sec. 111. Effect on other laws

"(a) This title does not annul, alter, or affect, or exempt any creditor from complying with, the laws of any State relating to the disclosure of information in connection with credit transactions, except to the extent that those laws are inconsistent with the provisions of this title or regulations thereunder, and then only to the extent of the inconsistency.

"(b) This title does not otherwise annul, alter or affect in any manner the meaning, scope or applicability of the laws of any State, including, but not limited to, laws relating to the types, amounts or rates of charges, or any element or elements of charges, permissible under such laws in connection with the extension or use of credit, nor does this title extend the applicability of those laws to any class of persons or transactions to which they would not otherwise apply.

"(c) In any action or proceeding in any court involving a consumer credit sale, the disclosure of the annual percentage rate as required under this title in connection with that sale may not be received as evidence that the sale was a loan or any type of transaction other than a credit sale.

"(d) Except as specified in sections 125 and 130, this title and the regulations issued thereunder do not affect the validity or enforceability of any contract or obligation under State or Federal law.

"Sec. 112. Criminal liability for willful and knowing violation

"Whoever willfully and knowingly

"(1) gives false or inaccurate information or fails to provide information which he is required to disclose under the provisions of this title or any regulation issued thereunder,

"(2) uses any chart or table authorized by the Board under section 107 in such a manner as to consistently understate the annual percentage rate determined under section 107 (a) (1) (A), or

"(3) otherwise fails to comply with any requirement imposed under this title, shall be fined not more than $5,000 or imprisoned not more than one year, or both.

"Sec. 113. Penalties inapplicable to governmental agencies

"No civil or criminal penalty provided under this title for any violation thereof may be imposed upon the United States or any agency thereof, or upon any State or political subdivision thereof, or any agency of any State or political subdivision.

"Sec. 114. Reports by Board and Attorney General

"Not later than January 3 of each year after 1969, the Board and the Attorney General shall, respectively, make reports to the Congress concerning the administration of their functions under this title, including such recommendations as the Board and the Attorney General, respectively, deem necessary or appropriate. In addition, each report of the Board shall include its assessment of the extent to which compliance with the requirements imposed under this title is being achieved.

"Chapter 2—Credit Transactions

"Sec. 121. General requirement of disclosure

"(a) Each creditor shall disclose clearly and conspicuously, in accordance with the regulations of the Board, to each person to whom consumer credit is extended and upon whom a finance charge is or may be imposed, the information required under this chapter.

"(b) If there is more than one obligor, a creditor need not furnish a statement of information required under this chapter to more than one of them.

"Sec. 122. Form of disclosure; additional information

"(a) Regulations of the Board need not require that disclosures pursuant to this chapter be made in the order set forth in this chapter, and may permit the use of terminology different from that employed in this chapter if it conveys substantially the same meaning.

"(b) Any creditor may supply additional information or explanations with any disclosures required under this chapter.

"Sec. 123. Exemption for State-regulated transactions

"The Board shall by regulation exempt from the requirements of this chapter any class of credit transactions within any State if it determines that under the law of that State that class of transactions is subject to requirements substantially similar to those imposed under this chapter, and that there is adequate provision for enforcement.

"Sec. 124. Effect of subsequent occurrence

"If information disclosed in accordance with this chapter is subsequently rendered inaccurate as the result of any act, occurrence, or agreement subsequent to the delivery of the required disclosures, the inaccuracy resulting therefrom does not constitute a violation of this chapter.

"Sec. 125. Right of rescission as to certain transactions

"(a) Except as otherwise provided in this section, in the case of any consumer credit transaction in which a security interest is retained or acquired in any real property which is used or is expected to be used as the residence of the person to whom credit is extended, the obligor shall have the right to rescind the transaction until midnight of the third business day following the consummation of the transaction or the delivery of the disclosures required under this section and all other material disclosures required under this chapter, whichever is later, by notifying the creditor, in accordance with regulations of the Board, of his intention to do so. The creditor shall clearly and conspicuously disclose, in accordance with regulations of the Board, to any obligor in a transaction subject to this section the rights of the obligor under this section. The creditor shall also provide, in accordance with regulations of the Board, an adequate opportunity to the obligor to exercise his right to rescind any transaction subject to this section.

"(b) When an obligor exercises his right to rescind under subsection (a), he is not liable for any finance or other charge, and any security interest given by the obligor becomes void upon such a rescission. Within ten days after receipt of a notice of rescission, the creditor shall return to the obligor any money or property given as earnest money, downpayment, or otherwise, and shall take any action necessary or appropriate to reflect the termination of any security interest created under the transaction. If the creditor has delivered any property to the obligor, the obligor may retain possession of it. Upon the performance of the creditor's obligations under this section, the obligor shall tender the property to the creditor, except that if return of the property in kind would be impracticable or inequitable, the obligor shall tender its reasonable value. Tender shall be made at the location of the property or at the residence of the obligor, at the option of the obligor. If the creditor does not take possession of the property within ten days after tender by the obligor, ownership of the property vests in the obligor without obligation on his part to pay for it.

"(c) Notwithstanding any rule of evidence, written acknowledgment of receipt of any disclosures required under this title by a person to whom a statement is required to be given pursuant to this section does no more than create a rebuttable presumption of delivery thereof.

"(d) The Board may, if it finds that such action is necessary in order to permit homeowners to meet bona fide personal financial emergencies, prescribe regulations authorizing the modification or waiver of any rights created under this section to the extent and under the circumstances set forth in those regulations.

"(e) This section does not apply to the creation or retention of a first lien against a dwelling to finance the acquisition of that swelling.

"Sec. 126. Content of periodic statements

"If a creditor transmits periodic statements in connection with any extension of consumer credit other than under an open end consumer credit plan, then each of those statements shall set forth each of the following items:

"(1) The annual percentage rate of the total finance charge.

"(2) The date by which, or the period (if any) within which, payment must be made in order to avoid additional finance charges or other charges.

"(3) Such of the items set forth in section 127 (b) as the Board may by regulation require as appropriate to the terms and conditions under which the extension of credit in question is made.

"Sec. 127. Open end consumer credit plans

"(a) Before opening any account under an open end consumer credit plan, the creditor shall disclose to the person to whom credit is to be extended each of the following items, to the extent applicable:

"(1) The conditions under which a finance charge may be imposed, including the time period, if any, within which any credit extended may be repaid without incurring a finance charge.

"(2) The method of determining the balance upon which a finance charge will be imposed.

"(3) The method of determining the amount of the finance charge, including any minimum or fixed amount imposed as a finance charge.

"(4) Where one or more periodic rates may be used to compute the finance charge, each such rate, the range of balances to which it is applicable, and the corresponding nominal annual percentage rate determined by multiplying the periodic rate by the number of periods in a year.

"(5) If the creditor so elects,

"(A) the average effective annual percentage rate of return received from accounts under the plan for a representative period of time; or

"(B) whenever circumstances are such that the computation of a rate under subparagraph (A) would not be feasible or practical, or would be misleading or meaningless, a projected rate of return to be received from accounts under the plan.

"The Board shall prescribe regulations, consistent with commonly accepted standards for accounting or statistical procedures, to carry out the purposes of this paragraph.

"(6) The conditions under which any other charges may be imposed, and the method by which they will be determined.

"(7) The conditions under which the creditor may retain or acquire any security interest in any property to secure the payment of any credit extended under the plan, and a description of the interest or interest which may be so retained or acquired.

"(b) The creditor of any account under an open end consumer credit plan shall transmit to the obligor, for each billing cycle at the end of which there is an outstanding balance in that account or with respect to which a finance charge is imposed, a statement setting forth each of the following items to the extent applicable:

"(1) The outstanding balance in the account at the beginning of the statement period.

"(2) The amount and date of each extension of credit during the period, and, if a purchase was involved, a brief identification (unless previously furnished) of the goods or services purchased.

"(3) The total amount credited to the account during the period.

"(4) The amount of any finance charge added to the account during the period, itemized to show the amounts, if any, due to the application of percentage rates and the amount, if any, imposed as a minimum or fixed charge.

"(5) Where one or more periodic rates may be used to compute the finance charge, each such rate, the range of balances to which it is applicable, and, unless the annual percentage rate (determined under section 107 (a) (2)) is required to be disclosed pursuant to paragraph (6), the corresponding nominal annual percentage rate determined by multiplying the periodic rate by the number of periods in a year.

(6) Where the total finance charge exceeds 50 cents for a monthly or longer billing cycle, or the pro rata part of 50 cents for a billing cycle shorter than monthly, the total finance charge expressed as an annual percentage rate (determined under section 107 (a) (2)), except that if the finance charge is the sum of two or more products of a rate times a portion of the balance, the creditor may, in lieu of disclosing a single rate for the total charge, disclose each such rate expressed as an annual percentage rate, and the part of the balance to which it is applicable.

"(7) At the election of the creditor, the average effective annual percentage rate of return (or the projected rate) under the plan as prescribed in subsection (a) (5).

"(8) The balance on which the finance charge was computed and a statement of how the balance was determined. If the balance is determined without first deducting all credits during the period, that fact and the amount of such payments shall also be disclosed.

"(9) The outstanding balance in the account at the end of the period.

"(10) The date by which, or the period (if any) within which, payment must be made to avoid additional finance charges.

"(c) In the case of any open end consumer credit plan in existence on the effective date of this subsection, the items described in subsection (a), to the extent applicable, shall be disclosed in a notice mailed or delivered to the obligor not later than thirty days after that date.

"Sec. 128. Sales not under open end credit plans

"(a) In connection with each consumer credit sale not under an open end credit plan, the creditor shall disclose each of the following items which is applicable:

"(1) The cash price of the property or service purchased.

"(2) The sum of any amounts credited as downpayment (including any trade-in).

"(3) The difference between the amount referred to in paragraph (1) and the amount referred to in paragraph (2).

"(4) All other charges, individually itemized, which are included in the amount of the credit extended but which are not part of the finance charge.

"(5) The total amount to be financed (the sum of the amount described in paragraph (3) plus the amount described in paragraph (4)).

"(6) Except in the case of a sale of a dwelling, the amount of the finance charge, which may in whole or in part be designated as a time-price differential or any similar term to the extent applicable.

"(7) The finance charge expressed as an annual percentage rate except in the case of a finance charge.

"(A) which does not exceed $5 and is applicable to an amount financed not exceeding $75, or

"(B) which does not exceed $7.50 and is applicable to an amount financed exceeding $75.

"A creditor may not divide a consumer credit sale into two or more sales to avoid the disclosure of an annual percentage rate pursuant to this paragraph.

"(8) The number, amount, and due dates or periods of payments scheduled to repay the indebtedness.

"(9) The default, delinquency, or similar charges payable in the event of late payments.

"(10) A description of any security interest held or to be retained or identification of the property to which the security interest relates.

"(b) Except as otherwise provided in this chapter, the disclosures required under subsection (a) shall be made before the credit is extended, and may be made by disclosing the information in the contract or other evidence of indebtedness to be signed by the purchaser.

"(c) If a creditor receives a purchase order by mail or telephone without personal solicitation, and the cash price and the deferred payment price and the terms of financing, including the annual percentage rate, are set forth in the creditor's catalog or other printed material distributed to the public, then the disclosures required under subsection (a) may be made at any time not later than the date the first payment is due.

"(d) If a consumer credit sale is one of a series of consumer credit sales transactions made pursuant to an agreement providing for the addition of the deferred payment price of that sale to an existing outstanding balance, and the person to whom the credit is extended has approved in writing both the annual percentage rate or rates and the method of computing the finance charge or charges, and the creditor retains no security interest in any property as to which he has received payments aggregating the amount of the sales price including any finance charges attributable thereto, then the disclosure required under subsection (a) for the particular sale may be made at any time not later than the date the first payment for that sale is due. For the purposes of this subsection, in the case of items purchased on different dates, the first purchased shall be deemed first paid for, and in the case of items purchased on the same date, the lowest priced shall be deemed first paid for.

"Sec. 129. Consumer loans not under open end credit plans

"(a) Any creditor making a consumer loan or otherwise extending consumer credit in a transaction which is neither a consumer credit sale nor under an open end consumer credit plan shall disclose each of the following items, to the extent applicable:

"(1) The amount of credit of which the obligor will have the actual use, or which is or will be paid to him or for his account or to another person on his behalf.

"(2) All charges, individually itemized, which are included in the amount of credit extended but which are not part of the finance charge.

"(3) The total amount to be financed (the sum of the amounts referred to in paragraph (1) plus the amounts referred to in paragraph (2)).

"(4) Except in the case of a loan secured by a first lien on a dwelling and made to finance the purchase of that dwelling, the amount of the finance charge.

"(5) The finance charge expressed as an annual percentage rate except in the case of a finance charge.

"(A) which does not exceed $5 and is applicable to an extension of consumer credit not exceeding $75, or

"(B) which does not exceed $7.50 and is applicable to an extension of consumer credit exceeding $75.

"A creditor may not divide an extension of credit into two or more transactions to avoid the disclosure of an annual percentage rate pursuant to this paragraph.

"(6) The number, amount, and the due dates or periods of payments scheduled to repay the indebtedness.

"(7) The default, delinquency, or similar charges payable in the event of late payments.

"(8) A description of any security interest held or to be retained or acquired by the creditor in connection with the extension of credit, and a clear identification of the property to which the security interest relates.

"(b) Except as otherwise provided in this chapter, the disclosures required by subsection (a) shall be made before the credit is extended, and may be made by disclosing the information in the note or other evidence of indebtedness to be signed by the obligor.

"(c) If a creditor receives a request for an extension of credit by mail or telephone without personal solicitation and the terms of financing, including the annual percentage rate for representative amounts of credit, are set forth in the creditor's printed material distributed to the public, or in the contract of loan or other printed material delivered to the obligor, then the disclosures required under subsection (a) may be made at any time not later than the date the first payment is due.

"Sec. 130. Civil liability

"(a) Except as otherwise provided in this section, any creditor who fails in connection with any consumer credit transaction to disclose to any person any information required under this chapter to be disclosed to that person is liable to that person in an amount equal to the sum of

"(1) twice the amount of the finance charge in connection with the transaction, except that the liability under this paragraph shall not be less than $100 nor greater than $1,000; and

"(2) in the case of any successful action to enforce the foregoing liability, the costs of the action together with a reasonable attorney's fee as determined by the court.

"(b) A creditor has no liability under this section if within fifteen days after discovering an error, and prior to the institution of an action under this section or the receipt of written notice of the error, the creditor notifies the person concerned of the error and makes whatever adjustments in the appropriate account are necessary to insure that the person will not be required to pay a finance charge in excess of the amount or percentage rate actually disclosed.

"(c) A creditor may not be held liable in any action brought under this section for a violation of this chapter if the creditor shows by a preponderance of evidence that the violation was not intentional and resulted from a bona fide error notwithstanding the maintenance of procedures reasonably adapted to avoid any such error.

"(d) Any action which may be brought under this section against the original creditor in any credit transaction involving a security interest in real property may be maintained against any subsequent assignee of the original creditor where the assignee, its subsidiaries, or affiliates were in a continuing business relationship with the original creditor either at the time the credit was extended or at the time of the assignment, unless the assignment was involuntary, or the assignee shows by a preponderance of evidence that it did not have reasonable grounds to believe that the original creditor was engaged in violations of this chapter, and that it maintained procedures reasonably adapted to apprise it of the existence of any such violations.

"(e) Any action under this section may be brought in any United States district court, or in any other court of competent jurisdiction, within one year from the date of the occurrence of the violation.

"Sec. 131. Written acknowledgment as proof of receipt

"Except as provided in section 125 (c) and except in the case of actions brought under section 130 (d), in any action or proceeding by or against any subsequent assignee of the original creditor without knowledge to the contrary by the assignee when he acquires the obligation, written acknowledgment of receipt by a person to whom a statement is required to be given pursuant to this title shall be conclusive proof of the delivery thereof and, unless the violation is apparent on the face of the delivery thereof and, unless the violation is apparent on the face of the statement, of compliance with this chapter. This section does not affect the rights of the obligor in any action against the original creditor.

"Chapter 3—Credit Advertising

"Sec. 141. Catalogs and multiple-page advertisements

"For the purposes of this chapter, a catalog or other multiple-page advertisement shall be considered a single advertisement if it clearly and conspicuously displays a credit terms table on which the information required to be stated under this chapter is clearly set forth.

"Sec. 142. Advertising of downpayments and installments

"No advertisement to aid, promote, or assist directly or indirectly any extension of consumer credit may state

"(1) that a specific periodic consumer credit amount or installment amount can be arranged, unless the creditor usually and customarily arranges credit payments or installments for that period and in that amount.

"(2) that a specified downpayment is required in connection with any extension of consumer credit, unless the creditor usually and customarily arranges downpayments in that amount.

"Sec. 143. Advertising of open end credit plans

"No advertisement to aid, promote, or assist directly or indirectly the extension of consumer credit under an open end credit plan may set forth any of the specific terms of that plan or the appropriate rate determined under section 127 (a) (5) unless it also clearly and conspicuously sets forth all of the following items:

"(1) The time period, if any, within which any credit extended may be repaid without incurring a finance charge.

"(2) The method of determining the balance upon which a finance charge will be imposed.

"(3) The method of determining the amount of the finance charge, including any minimum or fixed amount imposed as a finance charge.

"(4) Where periodic rates may be used to compute the finance charge, the periodic rates expressed as annual percentage rates.

"(5) Such other or additional information for the advertising of open end credit plans as the Board may by regulation require to provide for adequate comparison of credit costs as between different types of open end credit plans.

"Sec. 144. Advertising of credit other than open end plans

"(a) Except as provided in subsection (b), this section applies to any advertise-

ment to aid, promote, or assist directly or indirectly any consumer credit sale, loan, or other extension of credit subject to the provisoes of this title, other than open end credit plan.

"(b) The provisions of this section do not apply to advertisements of residential real estate except to the extent that the Board may by regulation require.

"(c) If any advertisement to which this section applies states the rate of a finance charge, the advertisement shall state the rate of that charge expressed as an annual percentage rate.

"(d) If any advertisement to which this section applies states the amount of the downpayment, if any, the amount of any installment payment, the dollar amount of any finance charge, or the number of installments or the period of repayment, then the advertisement shall state all of the following items:

"(1) The cash price or the amount of the loan as applicable.

"(2) The downpayment, if any.

"(3) The number, amount, and due dates or period of payments scheduled to repay the indebtedness if the credit is extended.

"(4) The rate of the finance charge expressed as an annual percentage rate.

"Sec. 145. Nonliability of media

"There is no liability under this chapter on the part of any owner or personnel, as such, of any medium in which an advertisement appears or through which it is disseminated."